Loss of Biodiversity

EXPLORING ENVIRONMENTAL CHALLENGES
A MULTIDISCIPLINARY APPROACH

SERIES EDITORS

Sharon L. Spray, Assistant Professor of Political Science Elon University
Karen L. McGlothlin, Assistant Professor of Biology The University of the
South

ABOUT THE SERIES

Exploring Environmental Challenges: A Multidisciplinary Approach is a
series of short readers designed for introductory-level, interdisciplinary
environmental sciences, or environmental studies courses. Each reader, focused on a single, complex topic of environmental concern, outlines the
concepts, methods, and current research approaches used in the study of
that particular environmental challenge from six distinct fields of study in
the natural sciences, social sciences, and humanities. This approach en-
ables students and faculty alike to become familiar with a topic from perspectives outside their own training and to develop a broader appreciation
of the breadth of efforts involved in investigating select, complex environmental issues.

TITLES IN SERIES

Global Climate Change, Sharon L. Spray and Karen L. McGlothlin
Loss of Biodiversity, Sharon L. Spray and Karen L. McGlothlin
Wetlands, Sharon L. Spray and Karen L. McGlothlin

Exploring
Environmental
Challenges

A MULTIDISCIPLINARY
APPROACH

Loss of Biodiversity

EDITED BY
Sharon L. Spray & Karen L. McGlothlin

ROWMAN & LITTLEFIELD PUBLISHERS, INC.
Lanham • Boulder • New York • Toronto • Oxford

ROWMAN & LITTLEFIELD PUBLISHERS, INC.

Published in the United States of America
by Rowman & Littlefield Publishers, Inc.
A wholly owned subsidary of The Rowman & Littlefield Publishing Group, Inc.
4501 Forbes Boulevard, Suite 200, Lanham, Maryland 20706
www.rowmanlittlefield.com

PO Box 317
Oxford
OX2 9RU, UK

British Library Cataloguing in Publication Information Available

Library of Congress Cataloging-in-Publication Data

Loss of biodiversity / edited by Sharon L. Spray and Karen L.
McGlothlin.
    p. cm. — (Exploring environmental challenges)
Includes bibliographical references and index.
    ISBN 0-7425-2566-X (alk. paper) — ISBN 0-7425-2567-8 (pbk. : alk.
paper)
    1. Biological diversity conservation. I. Spray, Sharon L. II.
McGlothlin, Karen L. (Karen Leah) III. Series.
    QH75.L64 2003
    333.95'16—dc22
                       2003018355

Printed in the United States of America

♾™ The paper used in this publication meets the minimum requirements of American
National Standard for Information Sciences—Permanence of Paper for Printed Library
Materials, ANSI/NISO Z39.48-1992.

Contents

About the Contributors   vii

Preface   ix

Introduction   xiii
    Sharon L. Spray and Karen L. McGlothlin

1 LIFE LINES   3
    A Geoscience Perspective on Historical Losses
    of Biodiversity
    David H. Backus

2 A CHANGING BALANCE   29
    An Ecological Perspective on the Loss of Biodiversity
    J. Whitfield Gibbons and Karen L. McGlothlin

3 DIMINISHING SONGBIRDS   55
    A Conservation Biology Case Study of
    Eastern Songbirds
    David G. Haskell

4 VALUING NATURE   75
    Ethical Perspectives on the Loss of Biodiversity
    Ben A. Minteer

5 PRICING PROTECTION   99
    Understanding the Environmental Economics
    of Biodiversity Protection
    David A. Anderson

6 THE POLITICS OF BIODIVERSITY   119
A Political Case Study of the Endangered Species Act
Alan Balch and Daniel Press

7 THE GLOBAL CHALLENGE   149
Concluding Thoughts on the Loss of Biodiversity
Sharon L. Spray and Karen L. McGlothlin

Glossary   *163*
Index   *175*

About the Contributors

Dr. David A. Anderson is the Paul G. Blazer Associate Professor of Economics at Centre College in Danville, Kentucky, where he teaches courses in environmental economics and other areas of economic study. He is the author of more than two dozen journal articles and book chapters as well as the textbook *Environmental Economics and Natural Resource Management*, published by South-Western College Publishing.

Mr. Alan Balch is a Ph.D. candidate in the Department of Environmental Studies at the University of California, Santa Cruz. His focus is on political economy and sustainability, paying particular attention to U.S. environmental policy (both national and local), biodiversity protection, solid waste management, and resource efficient consumption and production patterns. He holds an M.S. in environmental science and a B.A. in biology.

Dr. J. Whitfield Gibbons received his M.S. in biology from the University of Alabama and his Ph.D. in zoology from Michigan State University. He is currently a professor of ecology at the University of Georgia's Savannah River Ecology Laboratory, where he is head of the Environmental Outreach and Education Program. He is actively involved in conservation efforts nationally through Partners in Amphibian and Reptile Conservation (PARC).

Dr. David G. Haskell received his B.S. in zoology from Oxford University and his Ph.D. in ecology and evolutionary biology from Cornell University. He is an associate professor of biology at the University of the South in Sewanee, Tennessee, where he teaches classes in ecology, evolution, ornithology, and environmental studies. His research examines the conservation of biodiversity in Tennessee and the evolution of animal behavior.

Dr. Karen L. McGlothlin received her M.S. in biological sciences from East Tennessee State University and her Ph.D. in zoology from Clemson University. She is an assistant professor of biology at the University of the South in Sewanee, Tennessee, and teaches courses in invertebrate zoology, island ecology, entomology, and developmental biology. She is also an active participant in the interdisciplinary Environmental Studies concentration and in the Island Ecology Program.

Dr. Ben A. Minteer is an assistant research professor with the Human Dimensions of Biology faculty, School of Life Sciences, Arizona State University. He teaches and writes on environmental ethics, the philosophy and politics of environmental planning, and environmental history. He is the coeditor, with Bob Pepperman Taylor, of *Democracy and the Claims of Nature: Critical Perspectives for a New Century*, published by Rowman & Littlefield Publishers, Inc.

Dr. Daniel Press is an associate professor and a coholder of the Pepper-Gibberson Chair in Environmental Studies at the University of California, Santa Cruz, where he teaches environmental policy and politics. He received his Ph.D. in political science from the Claremont Graduate School in Claremont, California, and is the author of *Democratic Dilemmas in the Age of Ecology* (Duke University Press). He is also the author of a chapter titled "Local Open-Space Preservation in California," included in M. Kraft and D. A. Mazmanian's *Toward Sustainable Communities: Transitions and Transformations in Environmental Policy* (State University of New York Press).

Dr. Sharon L. Spray is an assistant professor of political science and environmental studies at Elon University in Elon, North Carolina. She earned her Ph.D. from the Claremont Graduate School in Claremont, California. In addition to teaching courses in American politics, international environmental policy, and domestic environmental politics and law, she serves as director of the Elon University Center for Public Opinion and Polling.

Preface

Sharon L. Spray
and
Karen L. McGlothlin

Exploring Environmental Challenges: A Multidisciplinary Approach is a series of short readers designed for introductory-level, interdisciplinary environmental sciences or environmental studies courses. Each reader, focused on a single, complex topic of environmental concern, outlines the
concepts, methods, and current research approaches used in the study of
that particular environmental challenge from six distinct fields of study in
the natural sciences, social sciences, and the humanities. This approach en-
ables students and faculty alike to become familiar with a topic from perspectives outside their own training and to develop a broader appreciation
of the breadth of efforts involved in investigating select, complex environmental issues. This series was developed to facilitate interdisciplinary

teaching in environmental studies programs by acknowledging that different disciplines bring distinctly different perspectives to the table and that scholars trained in those fields are best suited to explain these perspectives. The texts in this series are designed to assist faculty trained in a traditional social science, natural science, or humanities field to venture into areas of research outside their own training.

In the past decade, a rapidly increasing number of institutions of higher education across the country have developed a wide variety of interdisciplinary programs in both environmental science and in environmental studies. While many of these programs are centered primarily within the science curriculum, more and more institutions are strengthening their environmental sciences and environmental studies majors, minors, and concentrations by adding courses from both the social sciences and the humanities. The importance of integrating information from a variety of disciplines, including the sciences, social sciences, and the humanities, has been recognized and considered in the design and revision of environmental curricula. Liberal arts institutions, in particular, are moving toward the development of inter- or multidisciplinary approaches as a basis for their environmental programs. These approaches are as varied as the institutions themselves. While many programs offer team-taught courses to provide true interdisciplinary approaches, others are built around a series of courses from across curricula that address environmental topics. The foundation for and value of such programs is the recognition that complex environmental challenges will necessarily require strengthening the interface between the social sciences, humanities, and natural sciences if we hope to find productive ways of addressing these issues.

The concept for this series grew from discussions that emerged during the planning and development stages of an environmental studies program at the University of the South during the late 1990s. One of the points agreed on during our discussions was that all students enrolled in the environmental studies programs would be required to take an introductory course that would be interdisciplinary in nature and taught by a team of professors from the natural and the social sciences. In our case, that meant a teaching collaboration between a zoologist and a political scientist.

During the course of our conversations and explorations into the available literature, we found ourselves feeling a bit overwhelmed at the thought of teaching a truly interdisciplinary course. We felt that it would be difficult, at best, to hold classroom discussions concerning different concepts and approaches to the studies of various environmental topics from a variety of academic disciplines with our training centered in our particular fields. After much discussion, we decided that a series of edited readers, with each volume focusing on a single, complex environmental topic and chapters written by experts in various fields, would be of great use to students and faculty involved in interdisciplinary environmental studies programs. Thus, we began the development of this multidisciplinary series of readers on environmental challenges.

During the conceptualization stage of this project and later during the proposal review stage, the issue of "multidisciplinary" versus "interdisciplinary" teaching surfaced repeatedly. These two terms are frequently heard in discussions pertaining to environmental studies programs and often are used interchangeably. For this reason, we feel that it is important that these two terms be defined, providing, it is hoped, clarification for some and reassurance to others that a volume written from a multidisciplinary perspective can be used in an interdisciplinary course.

When we speak of multidisciplinary perspectives, we are referring to distinct disciplinary approaches to the study of a particular topic. Such perspectives do not preclude the integration of knowledge or material from other fields, but the interpretation of the information reflects a particular disciplinary perspective. We view this as a matter of disciplinary depth. As scholars, we necessarily cross the boundaries of knowledge and scholarship from other fields, but most of us have more depth in the field in which we received our academic training. Consequently, we interpret information through particular theoretical perspectives tied to our disciplinary training.

We view interdisciplinary teaching as the attempt at balanced integration of material from multiple disciplines. This, however, is a difficult goal when studying environmental issues. Most texts written about specific environmental issues reflect heavy bias toward the natural sciences with some discussion of policy and economics, or, alternatively, the focus may be in the opposite direction with an emphasis on policy and economics and limited discussion of science. More problematic is that many of the available texts fail to incorporate in any meaningful way the work of humanists, anthropologists, or sociologists—areas we believe are essential for understanding complex environmental challenges.

The texts are purposefully balanced with half the chapter contributions from the natural sciences and an equal number of chapters contributed from scholars in the humanities or social sciences. Each chapter identifies important concepts and theoretical perspectives from each field, and each includes a supplemental reading list to facilitate additional study. We envision these texts to be the foundation for introductory environmental studies courses that examine environmental topics from multiple perspectives or other courses that seek an interdisciplinary focus for the study of environmental problems. Because we anticipate that students from a variety of majors, both science and nonscience, will use these texts, the chapters are designed to be understandable to those with little familiarity of the topic or the field about which it was written.

The series is not neutral in its basic premise. The various topics in the series were chosen because we believe that the topics addressed are environmental challenges that we want students to better understand and we hope work toward future solutions. Individual authors, however, were asked to provide objective presentations of information so that students and faculty members could form their own opinions on how these challenges should be addressed. We care deeply about the environment, and we hope that this series serves to stimulate students to take the earth's stewardship seriously and promote a better understanding of the complexity of some of the environmental challenges facing us in this new century.

Introduction

Sharon L. Spray
and
Karen L. McGlothlin

Grizzly bears once roamed the land from the Mississippi to California, occupying territory from as far south as Mexico to as far north as Alaska. These magnificent creatures, highly adaptable to a number of geographic settings, were found in the western Plains, remote mountain regions, coastal zones, and wetlands during the 19th century. However, human settlement across the West placed considerable pressure on grizzly populations throughout the United States. Because grizzlies are omnivorous and are far more aggressive than other bears, they were feared by settlers and ranchers moving across the continent. By the end of the 20th century, trapping, hunting, and habitat loss had decimated grizzly populations in the lower 48 states, relegating viable grizzly populations to only a few remote wilderness regions in the mountain states of the West.

By the early part of the 20th century, grizzlies inhabited only 2% of their original range south of the Canadian border. In 1975, grizzly bears were listed as threatened in the lower 48 states under the **Endangered Species Act (ESA)**, but little progress was made in expanding grizzly populations in the years that followed. By the end of the century, the grizzly population in the lower 48 states was estimated at approximately 1,000, which were found nearly exclusively in fragmented islands of population in Yellowstone National Park, Glacier International Peace Park, and the Bob Marshall Wilderness regions of Wyoming, Idaho, and Montana.

The ESA, the world's strongest legal instrument designed to address species loss, provides the federal government with the authority to establish necessary conservation programs for endangered or threatened species, but such efforts have often faced considerable opposition because of conflicting goals for the use of natural resources. Efforts to recover grizzly populations throughout the West during the latter part of the century were stymied because grizzlies require vast expanses of wild, unfragmented habitat. Almost any effort to set aside large tracts of federal land for grizzly habitat inevitably conflicted with other federal land uses, including livestock grazing, logging, mining, and wilderness recreation.

During the 1990s, the U.S. Fish and Wildlife Service worked to overcome citizen and industry opposition to a grizzly conservation recovery program through the development of a historic citizen management plan. The plan called for the gradual reintroduction of the grizzly bear into Bitterroot-Selway and the Frank Church River of No Return Wilderness areas of Montana and Idaho (five bears per year for five years). Local residents, indigenous stakeholders, and industry representatives were involved in the plan's development, and a 15-member committee representing these interests was to be given oversight responsibilities for implementing the plan. The Fish and Wildlife Service also agreed to a modified designation of the grizzly as a nonessential, experimental population. This modified designation under the ESA allowed for more flexible management guidelines than what was allowed under the grizzly's previous ESA designation. Yet even with these innovative measures in place, the plan drew immediate adverse response from many industry spokespersons, citizens, and political leaders.

Timber and mining interests warned that an ecosystem protection plan would block resource extraction on federal lands and threaten local jobs. Many ranchers continued to oppose the grizzly reintroduction plan, claiming that viable grizzly populations would threaten domestic livestock populations in the region. Anecdotal comments written to the Fish and Wildlife Service on the recovery plan indicated that many residents of the region believed that humans would be at considerable risk of grizzly bear attacks under the reintroduction plan. Some of the comments suggested that the government was putting "bears before people," creating risks to hunters, recreationists, and residents. Others cited implementation costs, private property management concerns, and a fear that the plan could lead to restrictions on federal land uses, resulting in economic losses in the region.

Key political figures also opposed the plan. Idaho's Republican governor, Dirk Kemphorne, was perhaps the most outspoken. Kemphorne publicly assailed grizzly reintroduction efforts as a threat to citizen safety, a usurpation of states' rights to manage federal and state lands within state boundaries, and contrary to the interests of his state. Many of his concerns were echoed by both of Idaho's senators. The plan was still being debated when George W. Bush was elected president and his new secretary of the interior, Gail Norton, assumed responsibility for the implementation of the ESA. Despite years of planning and a concerted effort to involve multiple stakeholders in the development and implementation of a plan to protect an endangered species, the efforts of those involved ultimately could not withstand the pressure of this powerful change in the political environment. In June 2001, this historic citizen management plan to recover grizzly populations in the West was shelved without the opportunity to test this new approach to species protection.

The Loss of Biodiversity

For the past quarter of a century, scientists around the world have been documenting alarming rates of species declines attributable to human interactions with the natural world, but the development of politically acceptable mitigation strategies has proven elusive. The phrase **biological diversity**, or **biodiversity**, refers to the vast variety of life that occupies our planet—everything from the smallest bacterium to the largest blue whale. It also refers to genetic diversity, the variation in **alleles** (different forms of genes) and to **species richness** (the number of species of organisms occupying a geographic area). The maintenance of biodiversity is important for multiple reasons, including the formation of soils, the production of food, the purification of water, the breakdown or decomposition of waste products, the maintenance of the composition of gases in the atmosphere, and other important functions that contribute to the fundamental stability of **ecosystems.**

It has been estimated that, to date, there have been approximately 1.75 million different **species** of animals, plants, fungi, **protistans** (single-celled **eukaryotic** organisms), and bacteria (single-celled **prokaryotic** organisms) described on the planet earth. The discovery of new species that have been previously unknown to science occurs regularly. The fact that biologists continue discovering and describing previously unknown species of organisms indicates that there are many that have yet to be discovered, and there are estimates that the final species count for our planet may be as high as 75 to 100 million. Yet scientists are also documenting that many species are currently being driven to extinction at rates far greater than those that might be considered attributable to the natural processes, and this is causing great concern that many of the world's most valuable ecosystems are at risk.

Environmental pollution, global climatic changes, the introduction of nonnative species, overhunting, and habitat loss are among the list of factors contributing to species declines in both terrestrial and aquatic habitats. In some cases, these modifications are large scale. For example, the

World Resources Institute indicates that the world's forests, which provide fuelwood, protect water quality, store carbon, and are extraordinary resources for pharmaceuticals and industrial materials, are being harvested at unsustainable rates. "Almost a third of all watersheds have lost more than 75% of their original forest cover, and seventeen have lost more than 90%" (World Resources Institute 2001, 102) Mangrove forests, which are crucial for stabilizing coastlines and providing fuelwood for local communities and habitat for tropical fisheries, are some of the most threatened ecosystems. In some areas of the world, 85% of mangrove forests have been destroyed through wide-scale timber harvesting, shrimp farming, and coastal development (World Resources Institute 2001, 74).

Worldwide fish stocks are also facing critical levels of species depletions, much of which is attributable to overharvesting. The commercial marine fisheries industry, which uses a technique called **bottom trawling** to target economically valuable species (including shrimp, cod, and flounder), is responsible not only for the nonsustainable harvest of these organisms but also for the disturbance of over 14.8 million square kilometers of ocean bottom per year (Watling and Norse 1998). Using a bottom trawl, the target species is harvested, but species that are of no economic value whatsoever, referred to as **bycatch**, are also harvested. Species that may be destroyed as bycatch include **benthic** species such as sea stars, sand dollars, sponges, corals, and burrowing worms and **pelagic** species such as squid, jellyfish, and fish species that are not of economic value but are certainly of tremendous value in the marine ecosystem. The shrimp fishery provides a disturbing example of the extent of the damage that can be wrought as a result of the harvest of a single, economically important species. For every pound of shrimp purchased by the consumer, about seven pounds of "unimportant" marine life was destroyed and dumped back into the ocean during harvest (Safina 2001). Estimates of the total amount of bycatch killed during the harvest of economically important species each year range from about 25 million to 40 million tons (Pimm 2001).

While the unsustainable exploitation of organisms in a variety of habitats is producing widespread effects on biodiversity, many species are currently at risk because their populations are fragmented by human settlement and more subtle alteration of landscapes that disrupt migration patterns and long-term ecosystem viability. Grizzly bear populations in the mountain West fall into this category of biodiversity loss. Currently grizzly populations in the continental United States are divided into three geographic regions with limited numbers of reproductive pairs, resulting in restricted **gene pools,** which are the reservoirs of genetic variation for those populations. This isolation of disjunct populations increases the vulnerability of these existing small populations to decrease in **gene flow** as it decreases migration between populations, resulting in a reduction in genetic variation in individual populations. Populations that experience a marked decrease in the number of individuals are said to go through a **bottleneck,** which results in surviving populations that possess reduced genetic variability and are more genetically uniform. Genetic uniformity then opens those populations up to myriad other problems, including inbreeding depression and increased vulnerability to environmental change.

Efforts to increase grizzly populations in the West constitute an important illustrative example of the complexity that governments face in developing conservation programs to address both large-scale and subtle biodiversity disturbances. All conservation plans are based on the restricted use of ecosystems by human populations. Conservation programs that address individual species declines must also take into consideration a wide range of various interests that compete for use of many different resources within those regions.

In the case of the grizzly, the strongest resistance came from economic interests concerned about future limitations on the use of resources within the plan's geographic setting. In many cases, however, conservation programs clash firmly with the immediate needs of indigenous populations dependent on fragile ecosystems for food, fuel, and shelter. Without addressing issues of poverty, population growth, and unemployment, many of the world's conservation programs will be unsuccessful.

The benefits derived from conserving biodiversity are often less tangible than the immediate benefits (although often short lived) of job creation or resource revenues generated from extractive industries. This often results in greater weight paid to economic interests in policy decision making than species protection. In the case of the grizzly, the population was designated as "nonessential," giving greater flexibility to the management of the species under the ESA but making the argument to protect an endangered species more difficult to sell politically, especially in a region of the country that has been dependent on extractive industry jobs for decades.

Further complicating species protection are other political factors, such as government corruption and political greed, that have contributed to the overexploitation of resources in many of the world's most fragile regions. In other cases, inadequate resources for policy implementation and enforcement measures doom conservation policies to failure. In many cases, measures to protect biodiversity conflict with other societal needs, such as food production, job creation, and urban and industrial growth. There are also varying levels of ideological commitment to environmental initiatives and species preservation among political leaders who control the resources necessary to address environmental problems.

We realize that our discussion is an oversimplification of the obstacles inherent to species protection. What we hope to have conveyed is that the loss of biodiversity is not just a scientific problem. It is a social, political, and cultural problem as well. To understand the loss of biodiversity, one must go well beyond an understanding of causation to include an understanding of the social and political forces necessary to address this environmental challenge.

About This Book

The literature on the loss of biodiversity is as immense as the problem. Scientists, social scientists, and humanists have been researching and publishing information on this important issue for years. This book is structured to introduce readers to many of the concepts important for understanding the environmental challenge posed by the loss of biodiversity, discussing many of the obstacles addressed in the grizzly recovery example. Rather than focus on biodiversity losses of a particular region, species, or genetic trait, contributors to this book provide readers with an initial "tool kit" for understanding the multidimensional aspects of this environmental challenge and concepts central to their disciplinary perspective.

The book begins with chapters written by scientists followed by chapters from academics in the social sciences and humanities. Chapter 1 focuses on the loss of biodiversity throughout recorded time. This chapter is particularly important in understanding current losses in biodiversity given that many scientists have been warning for several decades that there is evidence to suggest that the world is losing its biodiversity of resources at alarming rates. But how does this rate compare to past periods of mass extinctions? One of the arguments typical of opponents of species preservation efforts is that the earth's biota are more diverse today than any other known period in time. But paleontologist David Backus points out that while there have been other geological eras in which our world underwent periods of mass extinction, the current period is unique in terms of the causes, the rates, and the relative impacts of present extinctions.

In previous periods of mass extinction, causation was believed to be tied to factors unrelated to human activity. Among the theories of causation for previous periods of mass extinction are asteroids, cosmic radiation, volcanism, predation, and climatic changes. But this is the first era in geological time in which a single species is radically altering the global environment. Backus points out that we are in the midst of a "new and radical ecological experiment in the history of life."

Ecologist Whit Gibbons and biologist Karen McGlothlin point out in chapter 2 that there are very immediate consequences for species loss. As ecosystems become less stable and species disappear, we jeopardize many of the **ecosystem services** we depend on to sustain and fulfill human life. Some of the services rendered by the vast array of living organisms include the production of oxygen, food, and fiber; the pollination of crops; the maintenance of water quality; and the regeneration of nutrients and production of chemical compounds used in approximately 25% of the prescription drugs in the United States (Tuxill and Bright 1998). The disappearance of seemingly innocuous species can have measurable consequences on our environment and the future of human populations.

Gibbons and McGlothlin also introduce readers to the concepts of island biogeography, habitat destruction and fragmentation, endemic species, some of the methods used to measure biodiversity, and examples of current ecological research pertaining to biodiversity. The concept of island biogeography, first put forth by MacArthur and Wilson (1967) regarding species on oceanic islands, is relevant to patches of terrestrial habitat, as seen in the case of the grizzly bear population in the United States. As illustrated in the example of the decreasing numbers of grizzly bears in the Northwest, the fragmentation of natural habitat leads to small "islands" of suitable habitat that can sustain only a fraction of the original bear population.

Chapter 3, a case study of songbirds by conservation biologist David Haskell, applies many of the concepts discussed by Whit Gibbons and Karen McGlothlin. Haskell's choice of songbirds to illustrate the challenges scientists and policymakers face in addressing biological diversity losses is a helpful one. The most obvious challenge to addressing biodiversity losses among bird population is the fact that bird populations are migratory. Unlike grizzly bear populations, which are contained within a relatively small geographic region, songbirds migrate over thousands of miles each year, and their populations are dependent on habitat throughout their migratory range. The survival of many songbird populations depends on habitat preservation in many nation-states with differing levels of resources, values, and interest among policymakers. Even though songbirds provide important ecological services, the intangibility of those services for most people makes prioritization of habitat and species protection elusive.

In the case of grizzly recovery, the habitat conservation discussion took on a different dimension than a discussion of conservation efforts for a socially valued and benign species such as that of songbirds. Some of the voices in the grizzly recovery debate asked whether there was any value at all in the preservation of a mammal that posed significant danger to human life. Although many environmentalists would suggest that the value of a grizzly or any other creature is unquestionable, the ethical debate about the intrinsic value of nature is far from decisive.

Within the environmental community, there are varying shades of diversity associated with the ethical debates concerning biodiversity preservation. Should we try to preserve all species? Are some species more valuable than others? How should we prioritize human well-being and species preservation? In chapter 4, environmental ethicist Ben Minteer provides an introduction to the current debate within the environmental ethics community, exploring various arguments that undergird conceptual as well as practical approaches to the valuation of nature in our policy choices. Minteer's work is not meant to promote one ethical stance over another; rather, his work is designed to provide readers with an understanding of the range and complexity of ethical arguments that permeate our policy discussions. We find this chapter extremely helpful in understanding the gap that sometimes exists between scientific understanding of environmental problems and the development of policy prescriptions.

The valuation of nature is also a concept central to the field of environmental economics and to policy decisions about species preservation. As we noted in our example of the efforts to reintroduce grizzly populations into select wilderness habitats in the mountain West, preservation efforts faced off with industries that sought use of the land for other economic purposes (grazing, mining, and logging). If preservation arguments are formulated around economic decisions, is it possible to develop successful policies that promote species protection? Chapter 5, by David Anderson, assists readers in understanding the major concepts and paradigms central to economic analyses used in environmental policymaking. Whether one agrees or disagrees with using economic concepts as the basis for species preservation, economic approaches remain central to policy formation. Anderson's chapter discusses the strengths and weaknesses of cost-benefit analyses, the role uncertainty plays in environmental valuation, market failures, and other important economic concepts central to understanding policy development.

As illustrated with the case of grizzly bear recovery, political factors weigh heavily in biodiversity protection efforts. In chapter 6, to help readers understand the political dynamics that shape environmental policy, political scientists Daniel Press and Alan Balch provide a case study of the ESA. Although not necessarily typical of the politics surrounding biodiversity losses in other countries, the history of the ESA is worth exploration given that it is considered the strongest national policy to address the loss of biodiversity of any nation in the world. In addition, the persistent controversies that have occurred over time as this important policy has been used highlight the strengths and limitations of policies that address the loss of biodiversity on a species-by-species basis.

The politics of preservation under the ESA raise important questions about the viability of stabilizing biodiversity losses throughout the world. In chapter 7, we briefly discuss the difficulty the world community faces when trying to address the loss of biodiversity throughout the world. Efforts to curb losses in biodiversity on a global scale will ultimately be even more difficult to address than it has been in the United States, which has substantially more resources for addressing this issue than other nations. Efforts to address the loss of biodiversity on a global scale will be faced with unraveling the layers of complexity associated with transboundary cooperative efforts, including differing levels of economic development, poverty, population pressures, and other factors that strongly affect conservation efforts.

Certainly not all disciplines or perspectives on the issue of biodiversity losses are included in this volume, nor is the order of chapter meant to convey the message that one perspective is more important than another. Chapters can be read individually or sequentially. All chapters are purposefully designed to highlight major concepts that can be applied in further exploration of the challenge and consequences of the declining diversity of life.

xxivSHARON L. SPRAY AND KAREN L. McGLOTHLIN

REFERENCES

MacArthur, R., and E. O. Wilson. 1967. *The theory of island biogeography.* Princeton, N.J.: Princeton University Press.

Pimm, S. L. 2001. *The world according to Pimm: A scientist audits the earth.* New York: McGraw-Hill.

Safina, C. 2001. The Audubon guide to seafood. In *The biodiversity crisis: Losing what counts.* Edited by M. Navacek. New York: New Press, 26–31.

Tuxhill, J., and C. Bright. 1998. Losing strands in the web of life. In *State of the world 1998: A Worldwatch Institute report on progress toward a sustainable society.* Edited by L. R. Brown et al. New York: Norton, 41–58.

Watling, J., and E. Norse. 1998. Disturbance of the seabed by mobile fishing gear: A comparison to forest clearcutting. *Conservation Biology* 12(6):1180–97.

World Resources Institute. 2001. *World Resources 2000–2001: People and Ecosystems: The Fraying Web of Life.* Washington, D.C.: World Resources Institute.

SUGGESTED READINGS

IUCN—World Conservation Union. 2002. The IUCN Red List of Threatened Species™. http://redlist.org.

Regan, H. M. 2001. The currency and tempo of extinction. *American Naturalist* 157(1):1–10.

Wilson, E. O. 2002. *The future of life.* New York: Knopf.

Loss of Biodiversity

Life Lines

A GEOSCIENCE
PERSPECTIVE
ON HISTORICAL
LOSSES OF
BIODIVERSITY

David H. Backus

In our ability to extract and consume the world's resources, *Homo sapiens* is without peer in the history of life on earth. The technological abilities of our species have allowed us to mold the environment for our use, a complete reversal of the usual relationship between an organism and its environment. Consequently, humans are also unique in the history of the world in their ability to destroy other species.

There have been five great mass killings of species (**mass extinction events**) in the history of the earth. The dinosaurs (except birds) are the most famous victims of the fifth great mass killing that took place about 65 million years ago (mya) at the end of the **Cretaceous period**. Many scientists who study the biodiversity of the earth today believe that humans in the past and today are causing the sixth great mass killing of species in earth history through hunting, habitat destruction, and climate change. The most controversial in this trio is **global climate change**. The amount of carbon dioxide (CO_2) being adding to the atmosphere by human activity increases daily. Higher levels of **greenhouse gases** (particularly CO_2) in the atmosphere have the potential to cause a warming of the earth's climate and altering its biodiversity and ecosystems. It is not clear how fast or drastic the effects on our planet will be as the composition of our atmosphere changes, yet it has long been proposed that climate change is the main culprit in all the earth's past mass extinctions.

What causes extinction? Are mass killings (extinction of greater than 50% of species) different in some way from normal extinction? What is the duration of an extinction event? Has climate change caused mass extinction in the past? What effect has extinction had on the earth's biodiversity through time?

Over the past three decades, paleontologists and other geoscientists have been looking more closely at the fossil record in order to answer these and other fundamental questions about the history of life on our planet. One of the principle ideas that has driven the study of geology over the past 200 years is that the present is the key to the past. However, it is now clear that the earth's biological and climatic history is the key to the present, as past extinction events are now the benchmarks for evaluating our current biotic crises.

How Extinction Is Studied

THE STUDY OF EARTH SYSTEMS: PROBLEMS

The study of the history of life on earth can be compared to putting together a large, complicated puzzle with two-thirds of the pieces missing and no box cover. Paleontologists make up the subset of geoscientists who study the fossil record. Here are some of the problems they face:

1. Soft-bodied animals do not often preserve well. This means that the fossil record is heavily biased toward animals with hard parts (shells

and bones). There are cases of exceptional preservation in the fossil record, such as the **Burgess Shale** of middle **Cambrian period** (about 520 mya). These special deposits represent extremely valuable windows into the earth's biological past.

2. All environments are not evenly represented in the fossil record. Marine sediments that were deposited along the borders of continents are commonly found, while terrestrial and deep-sea environments are much less likely to be preserved in the rock record.

3. The history of the earth is not recorded consistently in the rock record. Some periods of time in earth's history are represented by a few meters of fossil-rich rocks, while other periods of time are represented by thousands of meters of fossiliferous rock. In general, younger periods of time are overrepresented compared to older rocks and their fossils.

Sedimentary rocks, rocks primarily deposited in or by water, can record chemical and hydrologic data as well as encase the remains of animals and plants. As the interest in studying global change in the geologic record has increased over the past several decades, new sets of problems have been encountered as scientists attempt to re-create slices of earth history from the ancient rock record. Among these considerations are the following:

1. The earth–moon system has evolved over the past 4.6 billion years. The length of the day was shorter 500 mya.

2. The orientation of the earth's axis has changed with time. In the Northern Hemisphere, the Tropic of Cancer moves closer or farther away from the equator, depending on changes in the tilt of the earth relative to the sun. The earth also wobbles like a top as it moves around the sun. In addition, the earth's path around the sun varies through time. These cycles of variation in the earth's orientation and orbit are responsible for the cycles of climate change that affect the earth today (**Milankovich cycles**). These cycles may have been different in the past.

3. The continents have constantly been in motion or changing their shape throughout the earth's history because of **accretion**, erosion and the movement of tectonic plates over the earth's surface. Some parts of the world were in the tropics at some times and near the poles at other times in the earth's history. These movements occur over hundreds of millions of years and affect climate and sea level.

4. The world's earth systems do not appear to have worked in the same way in the past as they do today. We are living in what is termed an "ice house" world, with ice caps at the poles, ocean circulation driven by cold-water production at the poles, low sea levels, and relatively low levels of CO_2 in the atmosphere. During other times, such as the Cretaceous period (144–65 mya), the earth was a "greenhouse" world with no ice caps, high sea level, high CO_2 levels, and ocean circulation driven by warm, salty water produced near the equator.

These complications have led to increasingly innovative and multidisciplinary approaches to assembling the puzzle pieces of the earth's past. Geoscientists now bring not just the traditional tools of careful collection and analysis of fossil remains, but an expanded tool kit that includes paleomagnetic data that are used for determining the position of the world's continents through time and the chemical analyses of ice and rock samples that produce records used to interpret climatic conditions in the past and to more precisely determine the time frame for global changes and extinction events in the earth's past. The study of mass extinction is no longer only for paleontologists; rather, stratigraphers, paleoceanographers, geochemists, and other geoscientists have pieces to contribute to the puzzle as we attempt to re-create the history of life on earth.

Linking specific causes to a particular extinction event in earth's history is hard to do. Geoscientists are often in the position of having to imagine the possible causes based on limited geochemical, paleontological, and sedimentological data. Here is a list of the most commonly proposed causes of mass extinction (in no particular order):

1. Sea-level change (rise or fall)
2. Climate change (cooling and drying)
3. Asteroids (rocks from space)
4. Changes in cosmic radiation
5. Chemical changes in the atmosphere
6. Chemical changes in the oceans
7. Volcanism
8. Epidemic disease
9. Predation
10. Competition from other species

Interpreting data in a single way or connecting data sets to a particular cause is difficult because the world's oceanographic, terrestrial, and atmospheric systems are connected, particularly through the movement of water in all its forms. Consider the following scenario for global change. A decrease in the amount of CO_2 in the atmosphere cools the earth, resulting in more ice at the poles and lowering sea level. In one sentence, we have identified three proposed causes of extinction. What would these changes look like in the rock record as recorded on land or in the ocean? How fast do these changes take place in the modern world or did so in the past? Many of causes in the previous list can have an effect on climate change in some way. Climate is not a simple thing; atmospheric circulation patterns, seasonality, and temperature are the best-known components. In addition, the position of the continents, the heights of mountain ranges, volcanism, and even asteroid impacts can affect climate. All these factors work at different time scales. Mountains develop and continents move over tens to hundreds of millions of years, while changes in the earth's orbit affect global temperature in cycles of 14,000, 22,000, and 100,000 years. Volcanoes and asteroid impacts throw gases and material into the atmosphere that can alter climate for a few years at most. Global temperature is the general gauge used to track climate change through time, but it should be remembered that there are many factors that affect climate and that they work on different time scales.

FOSSILS AND THE ROCK RECORD

To study the history of life on earth, you begin with the fossils. Not a single paleontologist does not have a favorite group of plants or animals. However, give a fossil to a paleontologist, and he or she should be able, with varying degrees of accuracy, to tell you the period of time in earth's history from which it came. Why? Because changes in fossil groups are the basis for telling time in rocks (sedimentary) where fossils are found.

One of the earliest geologic maps in the world was created in 1815 and was used in the exploration for coal deposits in England and Wales. Each distinct layer of rock described on the map was given a color, and included with the map were illustrations of the fossils found in each layer or formation. To link each set of fossils to a particular formation, the illustrations were printed on paper of the same color used to identify the formation on the map. This made it easy for any geologist looking for coal in a new area to go to an outcrop, collect fossils, and find out where they were in the local layer cake of rocks. The geologist would then move up or down through the cake to find the rock layer most likely to have a seam of coal.

Why did this map work? Because in each rock layer, a unique group of fossils could be found, and the fossil groups were always found in the same order. In this way, the fossils gave a relative age to each layer in the cake. The maker of this map was William Smith (1769–1839), and he was not a paleontologist. He had no explanation for why the fossil groups changed with time. He did not know the age, in absolute terms, of the rocks that he was mapping. However, he could use the relative position of the fossils he found to identify the rock layers that might contain coal—an important energy resource that our species was interested in using to fuel the **Industrial Revolution.**

At about the same time that Smith produced his map, it was recognized by geologists working across the English Channel in the Paris basin that the sequence of fossils found in the basin were not a continuous series. In particular, Georges Cuvier (1769–1832) described what he called a series of "revolutions" in the fossil record, where one group of fossil organisms was replaced by a new set of distinctly different organisms (Rudwick 1985). Some of these extinction events were clearly more profound than others. As studies of the fossil record continued in France and across Europe, these breaks in the fossil record became the boundaries for subdividing the entire sequence of sedimentary rocks that record the earth's biological history (see figure 1.1). The process of refining this relative time scale continues today as new geologic studies provide more information from around the world.

MEASURING TIME IN THE ROCK RECORD

Time is a key problem when it comes to linking causes to events recorded in the rock record. For instance, shifts in sea level (cycles of tens of thousands to hundreds of millions of years) work on a much different time scale than an asteroid impact and its effects (seconds to a few years). Earlier in this chapter, you were introduced to the relative time scale, which uses the relative position of fossils to organize a layer cake of rocks. However, linking the relative time scale ("this comes before that") to the absolute time scale ("this rock formed 24.5 mya ± 0.2 million years") can be a problem. The difficulty of defining a moment in time (extinction event) and putting a time scale on the chemical, biological, and sedimentological signals in the rock record is usually the root cause for much of the controversy at any extinction event. The suggested causes and their effects must work on the same time scale as the data recording the extinction event in the rock record.

Walter Alvarez, the scientist who first proposed that an asteroid struck the earth 65 mya killing the dinosaurs, based his idea on the presence of unusually high concentrations of the **element** iridium at the **Cretaceous/ Tertiary (K/T) boundary**. Alvarez was not looking for evidence of an asteroid impact when he made his discovery; rather, he was working on the problem of telling time in the sedimentary rock record. He was trying to find something in sedimentary rocks with an extraterrestrial source, a cosmic dust that rained onto the earth at a constant rate and accumulated in

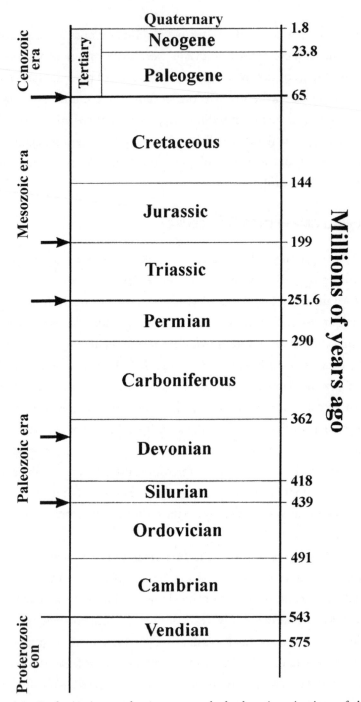

Figure 1.1. Geologic time scale. Arrows mark the locations in time of the five greatest mass killings in Earth history.

a predictable way. He did not find what he was looking for, but he nonetheless stumbled onto an interesting piece of earth history.

Creating a time scale in the sedimentary record depends on finding something on which to put a date. For example, volcanic **ash** and **tuffs** contain minerals with radioactive **isotopes** that can be analyzed to give a relatively precise date. There is always some error in the calculation, however. If several volcanic tuffs are found in a sedimentary layer cake that also contains fossils, the fossils and the rock they are found in can be assigned a time span defined by the age of the volcanics at the top and bottom of the fossil-rich layers. However, volcanic layers are not usually found right where you want them. Extrapolating between dated layers to put a time scale on each centimeter of rock between the dated units can be done, but this method has its hazards.

For example, at the Brazos River, Texas, the K/T boundary is directly overlain by a little more than a meter of boulders, gravels, and sands that resemble modern sediments deposited by giant tidal waves called **tsunamis** (Bourgeois et al. 1988). The Brazos River deposit is thought to be the result of a giant wave created by the impact of the asteroid that drove the dinosaurs to extinction. The meters-thick deposit at Brazos River was probably created within hours of the impact that, according to the best analysis currently available, occurred 64.98 ± 0.05 mya. The K/T boundary section at Zumaya, Spain, is easy to identify because of a sharp change in the color and the structure of the beds (Ward and Kennedy 1993). However, this section was deposited in a broad ocean basin where 1 meter of section may represent around 10,000 years. If you were tempted to divide that 1-meter section into 1-centimeter-thick slices, you would calculate that 1 centimeter equals about 100 years. Using this time frame, a fossil found 10 meters above the boundary might have been deposited 100,000 years after the extinction event. The calculation is made using what is called an average sedimentation rate. However, if we consider how the sediments were deposited at Zumaya, our age calculation does not turn out to be that good. Sediments that cascade into an ocean basin are usually pushed to the edge of the basin by large storms and ocean currents; they are not constantly pushed into the basin. There are periods of deposition, erosion, and nothing at all. Depending on the depth of the water and configuration of the ocean basin, sediment might be deposited every 100 to 1,000 years or longer. The thickness of each deposit is also variable. Each layer of sediment would range from a few centimeters to 1 meter or more in thickness. Periods of no sedimentation would result in small to significant time gaps in the record. In addition, the absolute age measurements of the volcanic layers have error. All things considered, there is enough error associated with our age calculation to make it unreliable for measuring time in increments that are smaller than 100,000 years. There are places in the world where sediments are deposited under more uniform conditions (deep sea) where calculations of average sedimentation rate are more reliable for measuring shorter periods of time. There are also environments where the record is harder to interpret (terrestrial). Connecting the data from various environments is difficult yet necessary for a more complete picture of any event in the earth's history. Geoscientists continue to look for ways to improve the methods used to measure time in sediments.

ORGANIZING ORGANISMS

Every organism in the history of the earth that has been described by human scientists is given a two-part name, or **binomium**, that is unique to that organism. For example, the saber-toothed tiger from the last ice age in North America is named *Smilodon fatalis*. The first word (Smilodon) is the genus name, and the second word (fatalis) is the trivial name. Together, the genus and trivial names form the species name. In an effort to understand how all organisms on the planet relate to each other, each organism is then placed into larger groupings based on the characteristics it shares with all other organisms. This hierarchical classification scheme allows us to connect any species back to ever-earlier common ancestors through a series of more inclusive categories. In the case of the saber-toothed tiger *Smilodon fatalis*, it is placed in the family Felidae (cats), the order Carnivora, the class Mammalia, the subphylum Vertebrata, the phylum Chordata, and the kingdom Animalia. Moving up in the hierarchy, you as a *Homo sapiens* are first grouped with *Smilodon* in the class Mammalia. Humans continue to be grouped with *Smilodon* at higher levels in the hierarchy but are not grouped with *Smilodon* below the class level. You should note that in this hierarchical classification system, there are more species than genera, more genera than families, and so on.

PATTERNS IN THE FOSSIL RECORD

To look at biodiversity through time, paleontologists begin by identifying the number of species present in one short interval in time, a snapshot of diversity based on outcrops of fossil-rich rock from around the world. Then the whole series of snapshots is put together, and the result is a movie of the history of life on earth, a movie in which humans appear seconds before the credits. This series of snapshots can then be analyzed using graphic or statistical methods.

The proliferation of personal computers in the 1980s gave paleontologists a new, powerful way to organize and manipulate the vast amounts of data that had been accumulating for over 200 years of study on the fossil record. Starting in 1981, University of Chicago scientist John Sepkoski published and refined a landmark analysis of data for all marine organisms described from the past 530 million years. In order to eliminate larger than acceptable errors in his data, Sepkoski's principle graphic shows biodiversity at the family level in the hierarchy of animal organization, not at the lower level of genus or species (see figure 1.2). In general, diversity increases through time; however, there are small to significant dips that show the effects of extinction events on this trend. Sepkoski's analysis also lumped the animals studied into three great evolutionary **faunas**. The Cambrian (Cm) fauna, the **Paleozoic** (Pz) fauna, and the Modern (Md) fauna emerge and replace each other in succession through time. It is clear that mass killings (extinctions) can have powerful effects on biodiversity. Note the sharp reduction in the Pz fauna and the

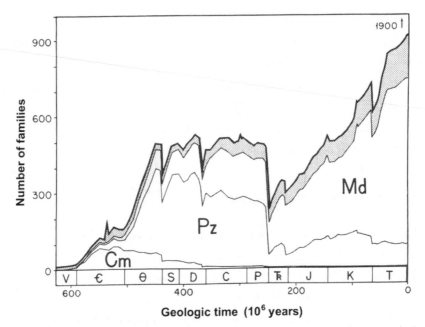

Figure 1.2. The three evolutionary faunas described by Sepkoski's factor analysis of Phanerozoic marine taxa. The analysis is of family diversity within classes. The faunas are the Cambrian Fauna (Cm), the Paleozoic Fauna (Pz), and the Modern Fauna (from Sepkoski 1984).

dramatic diversification the Md fauna after the Permian/Triassic (P/Tr) boundary.

Current Ideas on Extinction

It is now estimated that as many as 90% of all species and 60% of all genera living at the time went extinct at the P/Tr boundary. You should notice that using Sepkoski's diversity curve the effects of these extinctions are not as dramatic at the family level. If we look at the class level, only 4 out of 91 classes do not survive the extinction event. These kinds of distinctions will be very important to remember when we look at rates of extinction in the modern day and when considering the history of life on earth in general. For comparison, at the K/T boundary, where nonavian dinosaurs became extinct, it has now been estimated that between 65% and 70% of all species, 40% of all genera, and one single class of animals went extinct during that crisis, 65 mya. In both cases, these estimates will probably be revised down when new data become available. However, it is important to realize that when you look at estimates of the number of species going extinct today, the total number of species, genera, and families of organisms that exist today is far greater than at any time in the past. This means that extinction of 40% of species living today equals a much larger number compared to 40% species going extinct in the Cretaceous, the Permian, or any other time in the past. When you look farther up in the hierarchy, there have been very few new phyla since early in the Paleozoic (**Ordovician period**) and also very few new classes or orders created since that time. This is a very different picture from that predicted by Darwin's theory of evolution.

DARWIN AND THE HISTORY OF LIFE

There is no theory more influential in the study of earth history as Darwin's theory of evolution. As with any useful scientific theory, it has streamlined our understanding of how life on earth has changed through time, and it provides a basis for further discussion, argument, and experimentation. Most theories are subject to improvement or evolve over time. They would be useless otherwise. While the core ideas of Darwin's theory of evolution remain solidly supported, there are several of Darwin's ideas are not clearly upheld by modern analysis of the fossil record: the rates at which life has evolved, the origins of higher levels in the hierarchy of life, and that evolution is what might be termed a progressive force of nature.

At the time when Darwin was formulating his ideas (early to mid-1800s), geologists were debating the age of the earth (thousands vs. millions of years). That the earth could have existed for millions of years allowed Darwin to propose that new species were produced by the accumulation of small changes in existing species over very long periods of time (one species splits into two species). He used the same process to explain the creation of new genera as well as other higher-level groupings in life's hierarchy. For example, a group of species would become so diverse that it splits into two genera given enough time. Darwin believed that in this manner, life on earth evolved from the depths of early, lowly life (bacteria) to the lofty heights and the pinnacle of evolution: humans. As you can tell from the last statement, there is the implication of a progressive direction to evolution with humans as the logical (natural) end product of a long evolutionary process.

The fossil record does not clearly support these aspects of Darwin's theory of evolution. As described previously, the vast majority of animal phyla are already present by the early Ordovician. The pattern of the fossil record suggests that new species do not gradually appear through time but appear in bursts of evolutionary activity followed by long periods of quiet (theory of **punctuated equilibrium**).

When do these bursts of speciation occur? Great or small, these events usually occur when there are new ecological opportunities to exploit. For example, the great diversification of horses in the early Tertiary has been linked to the development of a new group of plants: the grasses. Driven by a cooling of the earth's climate, grasslands spread across large parts of the world. Horses developed better teeth for eating the new tough grasses and evolved modified feet for faster and more efficient locomotion to take advantage of this new ecological space. As grasslands spread, horses evolved from being small, many-toed forest dwellers to the large, long-legged, single-toed runners of today.

Another common way for ecological space to open up is through extinction. Extinction events clear out existing ecospace, which is then refilled by whatever animal or plant groups are available and quick enough to evolve and take advantage of the new ecological opportunity. After the available ecospace is filled, there appears to be little opportunity for innovation until the next crisis. The extension of this idea is that the greater the ecological change or disaster, the greater the opportunity for innovation. In the history of life, the occasional emergence of new groups of animals at the order and family level occurs after the larger mass extinction events when the ecological opportunities are greatest. Look again at figure 1.2, and you can see that prior to the P/Tr boundary, global diversity had hit a plateau. After the extinction and the severe reduction in the Pz fauna, global diversity rises dramatically, with a few setbacks here and there, throughout the Cenozoic era to the present day. Based on the most up-to-date analysis of the fossil record, it now seems that extinction is an episodic force in the history of life that creates evolutionary opportunities in what is usually a relatively ecologically static world. It should be emphasized that under usual ecological conditions, it does not appear that groups of animals (species, genera, and so on) can competitively force other groups into extinction. A group must be removed by an ecological disaster (small or large) before it can be replaced. A classic example of this idea is the extinction of the dinosaurs and the subsequent emergence of mammals after the K/T boundary. Prior to the extinction of the dinosaurs, mammals were unable to displace dinosaurs from their ecological prominence.

Unlike Darwin's idea of evolution as a progressive force in the history of life naturally leading to the evolution of humans, the fossil record appears to reflect a series of ecological disasters that allow for bursts of evolutionary activity followed by relative ecological and evolutionary stability. In addition, it appears that survivorship of these ecological disasters is not related as much to good genes, as Darwin would have predicted, as it is to good luck. As Stephen J. Gould (1989) reflects in his book *Wonderful Life*, the history of life is like any other history in that it is ruled by contingency. What if the asteroid that doomed the dinosaurs had missed earth? What if climate change had not created the African savanna and forced our ancestors from the trees? What if our earliest vertebrate ancestor *Pikaia* had not made it through the early Cambrian extinctions? Would *Homo sapiens* exist? As Gould relates at the end of his book, there are so many places for things to go wrong for the many ancestors of *Homo sapiens*. Rewind the tape of the history of life and play it over and over again a million times, and it is not likely that humans would ever exist again.

A profound implication of contingency in the history of life is that species that exist today are not necessarily more fit or inherently superior to species that lived in the past, as Darwin implied in his theory of evolution.

Rather, the earth's biota are more diverse today than ever before because, over time, animals and plants have evolved new ways to exploit the resources available on the earth. A principal way that opportunities for ecological experimentation are created is through extinction. We humans stand out as an organism not because we are more fit than any other species that has come before but because we have learned to exploit the earth's resources in ways no other species has done before. Humans do not now fit into the world's ecosystem as other organisms do but constantly try to change the environment to suit our needs. Humans are a new and radical ecological experiment in the history of the earth.

EXTINCTION: HOW IT WORKS

Here are some general ideas about extinction that are well supported by data from the fossil record and modern observation as outlined by David Raup (1991a):

1. The average time of existence for a species on earth is about 4 million years. Although, in some cases, old species do transform into new species, extinction is a reality for all life on earth.
2. Species with large populations are harder to wipe out than species with small populations. You have to eliminate all breeding populations to make a species go extinct.
3. Species that have large geographic ranges are harder to wipe out than species with small geographic ranges; unusual ecological stress is needed to drive geographically widespread species to extinction.
4. Genera with large numbers of species are harder to eliminate than genera with few species.
5. Extinction events that are recorded in many groups of animals must have been caused by stresses that cross normal ecological boundaries. For example, the dinosaurs (a terrestrial group of animals) and the ammonites (a group of marine animals) both went extinct at the K/T boundary.

Over the past few decades, research on extinction has generally concentrated on the larger extinction events. Each event appears to be for the most part unique, though there are also causes that are shared with other extinction events. There also appears to be cyclicity in extinction events during some periods of time in earth history (Cambrian period). It has even been proposed that major extinction events occur about every 26 million years. But there is no central cause that drives all extinction events. It appears that multiple causes for mass extinction is the rule rather than the exception. For instance, at the K/T boundary the combination is climate change and an asteroid impact. It is also probable that extinction events vary in their intensity so that there is a continuum between so-called **background extinction** and mass extinction events. The range of intensity in extinction events is comparable to modern phenomena, such as storms and floods, that vary in their size and frequency. There are storm seasons and springtime floods every year, but it is the major hurricanes and the 100- or 200-year floods that are remembered because of their impact on our lives.

Raup (1991b) took this concept a step further and produced a sort of insurance actuarial table for extinction events called a **kill curve** (see figure 1.3). Using the curve, you can see the average waiting time between extinction events of a given magnitude. The big five extinctions are approximately 100-million-year events, which means that chances are good that humans will not experience an extinction of this magnitude for a long time. However, this does not preclude the possibility that humans will be the cause of the next large mass extinction.

One aspect of mass extinction that may be a constant for all events is the occurrence of what is referred to as a "first strike." In effect, there is an ecological change that puts enough stress on a group of organisms so that their vulnerability to extinction is greatly increased. The story of the heath hen is an example of a well-known modern extinction event repeated here in an abbreviated form. The heath hen was a subspecies of the prairie chicken, which was common along the coastal regions of the eastern United States from Maine to Virginia during the 1700s. As a result of

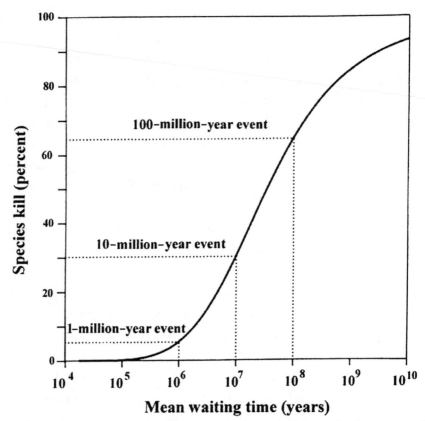

Figure 1.3. Kill curve showing the average waiting time for extinction events of various intensities (modified from Raup 1991a).

overhunting by humans, population numbers became smaller, and the geographic range of the heath hen became increasingly limited so that, by 1908, it was necessary to establish a 1,600-acre refuge on the island of Martha's Vineyard in Massachusetts to protect the last 50 birds. By 1915, the population was at 2,000 birds and growing. Then in 1916, a series of events drove the population toward extinction: A fire, spread by high winds, destroyed much of the heath hen's breeding areas and was followed by a very hard winter and an unusual influx of a predator: the goshawk. Later, a poultry disease introduced through domestic turkeys killed many remaining birds. By 1927, only 13 birds were left. The last bird was seen on March 11, 1932. Fire, predation, and disease are events that would normally have been no problem for the heath hen had it populated its usual geographic range. Unfortunately, humans caused the "first strike" by severely reducing the geographic range of the heath hen through overhunting.

CURRENT EXTINCTION NUMBERS

Humans are currently driving species to extinction primarily through the destruction of tropical rain forests. How does the impact humans have had on global biodiversity compare to mass extinction events in the past? Peter Ward (2000) has estimated that between 2,000 and 4,000 species of animals and plants went extinct during the K/T extinction event. Clearly, the fossil record is a poor reflection of global biodiversity from around 65 mya. It is probable that thousands to millions of species went extinct during the K/T event. However, let's compare these numbers with estimates of extinction for two animal groups that have more recent fossil records: birds and Hawaiian land snails. Using the work of Olsen and James (1984) and conversations with the authors, Ward (2000) suggests that more than 1,000 species of birds have gone extinct worldwide in the past 2,000 to 5,000 years. Approximately the same number of land snail species have gone extinct during the past 500 to 1,000 years in the Hawaiian Islands alone (Hadfield 1986). The decline of the Hawaiian land snail and the multitude of species that existed with them is due primarily to the conversion of upland forest to pineapple plantations. Each upland ridge is separated from its neighbor by a stream that is enough of a geographic separation that, over time, each upland ridge evolved its own species of land snail. Geographic isolation of a population is a significant step toward **speciation**, or the evolution of a new species. Islands, upland ridges, and even trees in a tropical forest can provide the necessary isolation for the evolution of new species.

It is estimated that 50% of the world's biodiversity is contained in tropical forests, which cover only 7% of the world's landmass (Myers 1988). Therefore, the conversion of tropical forests to agricultural and other uses

will have the greatest impact on global biodiversity. Janzen (1988) has calculated that 14,000 species of animals and plants can be found in the dry
forests of Costa Rica's Santa Rosa National Park. When dry forests are converted to banana plantations or utilized for other resources, 90% to 95%
of the species are lost (Janzen 1988). Myers (1988) has estimated that up
to 50% of species are lost when a large rain forest region loses 95% of its
initial diversity. This is because many groups, such as insects, have many
species that are found in only one forest type or that are associated with
only one kind of tree (Erwin 1988). One estimate of current extinction
rates in the tropics comes from Myers's (1988) work in the Brazilian rain
forest. He calculated that at least 50,000 species became extinct over a
35-year period as a result of logging and cultivation. This calculation suggests an extinction rate of close to four species per day.

Let's compare modern extinction rates with those calculated by Raup
(1991a) for the fossil record. As we noted earlier in this chapter, the average species exists for about 4 million years. If this calculation is redone excluding mass extinction events, the background extinction rate falls to
barely above zero (Ward 2000). A more conservative extinction rate for the
history of life on the planet is set by Myers (1988) at about one species per
year. Therefore, current losses in biodiversity due to the destruction of
tropical rain forests are hundreds to perhaps thousands of times higher
than the historical average for the past 500 million years of life on the earth
(Myers 1988; Raven 1988).

Projections of biodiversity loss in the future are even more disturbing if
current land use practices are not halted. Wilson (1992) suggests that a
20% loss in global biodiversity is possible by the year 2022 and estimates
current losses at 27,000 species per year. Calculations by Simberloff (1986)
on the potential loss of bird and plant species in New World tropical rain
forests suggest a decline in numbers of 69% and 66%, respectively, by 2050
to 2100. Simberloff concludes that the looming catastrophe in the world's
tropical forests is comparable in scope to any of the past mass extinction
events except for the Permian/Triassic crisis.

CLIMATE CHANGE AND EXTINCTION

The debate over climate change as an agent of extinction is an old one. The first documentation of an extinction event was a paper on the extinction of fossil elephants in the Paris basin by Georges Cuvier in 1796. Cuvier was later able to show that many other animals were included in the event and that the extinction occurred in a relatively short period of time (Rudwick 1985). This was contrary to the idea that extinctions were caused by gradual changes in climate and was proposed in a time when many geologists believed that all earth processes were gradual in their cycles of change. As a "catastrophist," Cuvier was a supporter of the idea that the earth was subject to sudden environmental disasters, whereas other geologists, such as Darwin, believed that earth systems changed very slowly through time ("gradualist"). Climate change is also appealing to humans as an agent of extinction because human life and survival have always been subject to the fluctuations of weather and climate. The debate continues today.

One of the advantages of studying climate change and extinctions in the **Pleistocene** is the relatively short period of time that has elapsed since the events took place. There has been less time for the deterioration and destruction of geologic evidence through the usual processes of chemical weathering, erosion, and global **tectonics**. There is also the advantage that most animals and plants living today are not very different from those that existed a few millions of years ago. Scientists reconstruct past climates using a variety of methods, known as **climate proxies**. Carbon dioxide and other atmospheric gases used to track climatic conditions can be measured directly from bubbles trapped in polar ice. The ice core record, which extends back more than 400,000 years, also records cycles in snow, tree pollen, sea salt, and dust accumulation. Marine sediments contain microfossils that can be analyzed for chemical isotopes (such as carbon and oxygen) that are useful for re-creating temperature, salinity, atmospheric CO_2, and other climactic conditions as far back as 180 million years. In some cases, tree rings and annual bands in corals provide a limited record of local environmental conditions. Complementing the climate data, human artifacts and fossils from as old as 40,000 years ago can be assigned an age using the carbon-14 **radiometric dating** technique, providing the information needed to calibrate the earth's climatic cycles. Calibrating cycles from ice cores and other data sources older than 40,000 years requires the use of other chemical isotope systems, such as potassium(K)-argon(Ar) and uranium(U)-lead(Pb).

Paul Martin (1984) has suggested that the cause of the Pleistocene extinction of large mammals and birds is human hunting (**overkill hypothesis**). He has connected the dispersal of humans throughout the world from Africa during the past 50,000 years with the disappearance of many large-bodied animals. Martin proposes that mammoths, giant bison, and other animals that were previously too large for human hunters to tackle became prey after the invention of large, fluted spear points made from stone, fitted to wooden shafts, and hurled using a throwing stick. He noted that extinction rates are more pronounced in areas of the world that humans colonized: the Americas, Australia, and the Pacific islands. He suggests that the large prey in these regions did not learn to fear these new hunters fast enough to survive the new threat.

Opponents of the overkill hypothesis suggest that climate change is the real culprit. They propose that as the climate warmed at the end of the last glacial cycle about 11,000 years ago, the seasons became more extreme (hotter summers and colder winters), making conditions intolerable for many plants and animals, especially the plant life necessary to sustain large-bodied herbivores such as mammoths and mastodons. The Pleistocene large-mammal extinction has been debated for about three decades with most new evidence unable to link the unusual pattern of large-mammal extinctions directly to climate change, although climate was changing in unusual ways at the time. It may be that, as with other mass extinctions, there were multiple causes. Perhaps the dual pressures of climate change and human predatory behavior caused these extinctions together. However, a recent review of the Pleistocene extinction debate by MacPhee (1999) suggests a consensus toward the idea that human predation is the cause. Another more recent study emphasizes the need to disconnect climate change as the default agent of extinction. A compilation of the best available climate and mammal diversity data from the past 65 million years shows no "linear relationship" between climate change and mammal extinction patterns (Alroy et al. 2000).

Looking back over the past 145 million years of record, the latest research suggests that the response of plants and animals to global change is highly variable. For example, plant and mammal distribution and diversity patterns are more closely linked to changes in rainfall, not to temperature. In contrast, changes in the diversity of marine animals, such as cephalopods (octopus, squid, and chambered nautilus) and echinoderms (sea stars, sand dollars, and sea urchins), closely follow fluctuations in sea level. There are also **pelagic** animals (ocean floaters and swimmers) whose geographic distribution and diversity patterns are more directly affected by changes in ocean temperature. In general, if an organism is not able to adapt to changing climatic conditions where it lives, it must either migrate or go extinct. Global change may favor one group over another. For example, lower sea levels in the Pleistocene allowed humans and other mammals to disperse into new regions around the world but also created problems for marine animals that lived along the edges of the world's continents.

Conclusion

Extinction has had a significant impact on the diversification of life throughout the earth's history. Extinctions large and small create ecological open space and opportunities for diversification. At several key moments in the earth's history, extinction events have opened the way for the evolution of new organisms, leading to significant increases in biodiversity. There are probably more species alive today than in any other period in earth history. It appears that extinction varies in magnitude from background levels up to the largest recorded extinction event at the Permian/Triassic boundary, although more work needs to be done on the lesser extinctions to firmly establish this idea. Individual extinction events seem to have multiple causes with larger disasters driven by global changes that cut across ecological boundaries. The puzzle for scientists working on extinction is finding new ways to link extinction events in the fossil record to some physical or chemical change recorded in the same rock. A primary problem for geoscientists researching events in earth history is telling time in the fossil and rock record. Earth systems, such as tectonics, climate change, and volcanism, work on different time scales.

The destruction of tropical forestlands is an immediate problem for global biodiversity. Unless deforestation in the tropics is slowed or halted, humans will be responsible for an extinction event comparable to any mass extinction event in the past with the exception of the Permian/Triassic crisis, the single largest extinction event in the history of the planet. Recent studies suggest that mammalian diversity patterns are not directly linked to fluctuations in climate over the past 65 million years. It is now considered likely that hunting by humans and not climate change is the cause of large animal extinctions in the Pleistocene. In this case, the Pleistocene extinctions are another example of how our ability to consume world resources puts other species in peril. Therefore, it seems that habitat destruction and hunting by humans has a far greater and immediate impact on current extinction rates than any potential problems related to climate change.

REFERENCES

Alroy, J., P. L. Koch, and J. C. Zachos. 2000. Global climate change and North American mammalian evolution. In *Deep time: Paleobiology's perspective.* Edited by D. H. Erwin and S. L. Wing. Supplement to *Paleobiology* 26(4):1–14.

Bourgeois, J. T., A. Hansen, P. L. Wiberg, and E. G. Kauffman. 1988. A tsunami deposit at the Cretaceous-Tertiary boundary in Texas. *Science* 241(4865):567–70.

Erwin, T. L. 1988. The tropical forest canopy: The heart of biotic diversity. In *Biodiversity.* Edited by E. O. Wilson. Washington, D.C.: National Academy Press, 123–29.

Gould, S. J. 1989. *Wonderful life: The Burgess shale and the nature of history.* New York: Norton.

Hadfield, M. 1986. Extinction in Hawaiian Achatinelline snails. *Malacologia* 27:67–81.

Janzen, D. H. 1988. Tropical dry forests: The most endangered major tropical ecosystem. In *Biodiversity*. Edited by E. O. Wilson. Washington, D.C.: National Academy Press, 130–37.

MacPhee, R. D. E. 1999. *Extinctions in near time: Causes, contexts, and consequences*. New York: Plenum.

Martin, P. S. 1984. Prehistoric overkill: The global model. In *Quaternary extinctions: A prehistoric revolution*. Edited by P. S. Martin and R. Klein. Tucson: University of Arizona Press, 354–403.

Myers, N. 1988. Tropical forests and their species: Going, going . . . ? In *Biodiversity*. Edited by E. O. Wilson. Washington, D.C.: National Academy Press, 28–35.

Olsen, S. L., and H. F. James. 1984. The role of Polynesians in the extinction of the avifauna of the Hawaiian Islands. In *Quaternary extinctions: A prehistoric revolution*. Edited by P. S. Martin and R. Klein. Tucson:. University of Arizona Press, 768–80.

Raup, D. M. 1991a. *Extinction: Bad genes or bad luck?* New York: Norton.

———. 1991b. A kill curve for Phanerozoic marine species. *Paleobiology* 17:37–48.

Raven, P. H. 1988. Our diminishing tropical forests. In *Biodiversity*. Edited by E. O. Wilson. Washington, D.C.: National Academy Press, 119–22.

Rudwick, M. J. S. 1985. *The meaning of fossils*. 2nd ed. Chicago: University of Chicago Press.

Sepkoski, J. J., Jr. 1984. A kinetic model of Phanerozoic taxonomic diversity. III. Post-Paleozoic families and mass extinctions. *Paleobiology* 10:246–67.

Simberloff, D. S. 1986. Are we on the verge of a mass extinction in the tropical rain forests? In *Dynamics of extinction*. Edited by D. K. Elliot. New York: Wiley, 165–80.

Ward, P. D. 2000. *Rivers in time: The search for clues to earth's mass extinctions*. New York: Columbia University Press.

Ward, P. D., and W. J. Kennedy. 1993. *Maastrichtian ammonites from the Biscay region (France, Spain)*. Memoir 34 of the Paleontological Society.

Wilson, E. O. 1992. *The diversity of life*. Cambridge, Mass.: Harvard University Press.

SUGGESTED READINGS

Archibald, J. D. 1996. *Dinosaur extinction and the end of an era: What the fossils say.* New York: Columbia University Press.

Chernicoff, S., H. A. Fox, and R. Venkatakrishnan. 1997. *Essentials of geology.* New York: Worth.

Erwin, D. H. 1993. *The great Paleozoic crisis: Life and death in the Permian.* New York: Columbia University Press.

Gale, A. 2000. The Cretaceous world. In *Biotic responses to global change: The last 145 million years.* Edited by S. J. Culver and P. F. Rawson. Cambridge: Cambridge University Press, 4–19.

Gore, R. 1989. What caused the earth's great dyings? *National Geographic* 175(June):662–99.

Jackson, S. T., and J. T. Overpeck. 2000. Responses of plant populations and communities to environmental changes of the late Quaternary. In *Deep time: Paleobiology's perspective.* Edited by D. H. Erwin and S. L. Wing. Supplement to *Paleobiology* 26(4):194–220.

Knoll, A. H., and R. K. Bambach. 2000. Directionality in the history of life. In *Deep time: Paleobiology's perspective.* Edited by D. H. Erwin and S. L. Wing. Supplement to *Paleobiology* 26(4):1–14.

Leakey, R., and R. Lewin. 1995. *The sixth extinction: Patterns of life and the future of mankind.* New York: Doubleday.

McGhee, G. R. 1996. *The late Devonian mass extinction: The Frasnian/Famennian crisis.* New York: Columbia University Press.

Paleoclimate review. 2001. *Science* 292(5517):657–93.

Pickering, K. T. 2000. The Cenozoic world. In *Biotic responses to global change: The last 145 million years.* Edited by S. J. Culver and P. F. Rawson. Cambridge: Cambridge University Press, 20–34.

Prothero, D. R. 1994. *The Eocene-Oligocene transition: Paradise lost.* New York: Columbia University Press.

Stanley, S. M. 1987. *Extinction.* New York: Scientific American Library.

www.bbc.co.uk/education/darwin/exfiles (BBC website on extinction and evolution).

www.pbs.org/wgbh/evolution/extinction (PBS website on extinction and evolution).

www.sprl.umich.edu/GCL/index.html (Global Change educational website).

2

A Changing Balance

AN ECOLOGICAL
PERSPECTIVE
ON THE LOSS
OF BIODIVERSITY

J. Whitfield Gibbons
and
Karen L. McGlothlin

The field of **ecology** is a subdiscipline of biology devoted to the investigation of the **species distribution** and **species abundance** of organisms within the environment and the relationship between those organisms and their surroundings. To most scientists engaged in **ecological research** that is directly applicable to environmental problems, the loss of **biological diversity**, or biodiversity, is the single most pervasive theme driving their investigations.

When one thinks about the term "biodiversity," it is easy to restrict those thoughts to the total number of species of plants, animals, fungi, bacteria, and other microorganisms in the environment. This, however, is an inaccurate representation of the entire picture that is biodiversity. The term "biodiversity" was coined in a chapter written by marine and forest conservation biologist Elliott Norse and included in a 1980 government report (Pimm 2001). The term has become commonly used to describe a concept that includes diversity on three levels. The most inclusive level includes **ecosystems**, which are **communities** of living organisms and the nonliving environment they inhabit. The second level includes **species**, which are groups of interbreeding or potentially interbreeding organisms found in ecosystems. Diversity can also be observed and quantified on a third level: the molecular. Biodiversity at this level is described in terms of **genes**, which are the segments of **deoxyribonucleic acid** (**DNA**), or the units of hereditary material passed from generation to generation. At this level, biological diversity is represented by the numerous genetic variations among members of even a single species (Wilson 2002).

Loss of biodiversity can occur at any of these three levels, and such losses are generally perceived as negative by ecologists. In recent summary works from a diversity of ecological fields, investigators have related their findings of species loss either through the decline in a particular **taxonomic group**, such as spiders (Horton et al. 2001), mollusks (Hallac and Marsden 2001), and reptiles (Gibbons et al. 2000), or in relation to an environmental principle or process, such as forest management (Noss 2001), river ecology (Ward and Tockner 2001), and the ecology of small, isolated wetlands (Semlitsch 2000). Clearly, quantifying and understanding the loss of biodiversity is a central theme of ecological research and of **conservation biology**, which is an interdisciplinary field devoted to the investigation and conservation of biological diversity at all levels through science, education, social, economic, and political means.

With the variety of research and the broad expanse of disciplinary fields involved in investigations concerning biological diversity and its conservation, the question that must be asked is, Why the high level of interest in biodiversity—what is the importance of biodiversity? Diverse reasons have been given in support of maintaining current levels of biodiversity, both for the best long-term interest of humans as well as for more esoteric, philosophical positions, and include ones based on religion, ethics, aesthetics, environmental stability, and untapped medicinal value (Gore 1992; Kellert and Wilson 1993; Odum 1971; Wilson 1992). Perhaps what has not been conveyed clearly enough to the public is that the maintenance of biological diversity is tremendously important to humans beyond reasons of aesthetics and ethics. Conserving biological diversity on an organismal level is important for the maintenance of **food webs**, which are defined as the sum total of feeding, or **trophic**, interactions occurring in ecosystems, and, ultimately, for the maintenance of ecosystems stability. Biological diversity is also imperative for the maintenance of genetic diversity, particularly when considering that the genetic diversity of agricultural crops and livestock has been restricted as a result of **selective breeding**. The preservation of a diversity of wild species that are closely related to crop species is important for providing reservoirs of genes that may be needed if climate change, newly emerging diseases, or other unforeseeable impacts damage or destroy agricultural species. Yet another reason for the conservation of biodiversity is the fact that there is no way of knowing which species of organisms might be valuable for providing future **ecosystem services**, such as the **biological control** of pests and the production of medicinal compounds (Bush 2000).

The intensity of public concern about the loss of biodiversity on local, regional, and global scales gains its force from attitudes that range from ones based on emotion to those based on solid research findings. However, even research ecologists often disagree among themselves about the best course of action in particular environmental situations, and a conservation position that some view as practical might be considered impractical by others. In situations in which natural habitats are to be modified and a loss of biodiversity is anticipated, solutions that address both environmental and economic aspects are often the ultimate compromise.

Research focused on biodiversity has a rich history that has progressed over the past two centuries from the earliest periods of natural history observations to **species inventory** and biodiversity **monitoring**. The classic, guiding theme of Andrewartha and Birch (1954) was to investigate the most fundamental concept within the field of ecology; that is, how can the observed patterns of the distribution and abundance of organisms be explained? Current studies that are related to concerns about the loss of biodiversity focus on numbers of species of organisms and the **abiotic** and **biotic** factors responsible for their distribution patterns. Thus, "biodiversity," although a relatively new term, is in no way a new concept, as biodiversity is merely a product of evolutionary, ecological, and other factors that determine the distribution and abundance of organisms.

Concerns regarding the loss of biodiversity have increased considerably in the past two decades, leading to unprecedented levels of research and publication that have focused on species loss in numerous taxonomic groups across many regions of the world. The information presented about the loss of biodiversity in books published since 1988 (such as Agosti et al. 2000; Dobson 1998; Donahue 2000; Gibbons and Gibbons 1998; Hubbell 2001; Hunter 1999; Novacek 2001; and Smith 2000) surpasses what had been written about the topic during the previous century. The loss of biodiversity has even been the driving force of globally significant legislation, such as the creation of protected natural areas in many countries, **Convention on International Trade in Endangered Species** (CITES) designations, and the passing of the Endangered Species Act in the United States. In addition, the year 2001 was designated as the International Biodiversity Observation Year with a goal of assessing and redefining our understanding of biodiversity on a global scale (Wall et al. 2001). Clearly, the permanent disappearance of species is disquieting to many people in both developed and developing nations.

An increase in public awareness of the concerns associated with losses in biodiversity is the result, in no small part, of high-profile examples of **extinctions** or near extinctions of some species of charismatic **megafauna**, such as the black rhinoceros, hunted to near extinction in Africa because of the value of their horns, or the elephant, whose numbers have dwindled as humans harvest their tusks for the ivory trade. While highly visible examples are valuable for raising awareness, it is also important that the public realizes that many of the organisms driven to extinction or to the brink of extinction are not charismatic species. In contrast, they may be species that are not particularly appreciated until their absences become devastatingly apparent, such as the eastern oyster in the Chesapeake Bay. This **keystone species** was overharvested for human consumption, resulting in a cascade of events that contributed to the drastic deterioration of environmental conditions in the bay itself and led to the corresponding economic losses that actually garnered widespread attention.

A variety of environmental impacts, both human and nonhuman induced, have been proposed and/or documented as leading to losses of biodiversity. Historic extinctions have been attributed primarily to environmental alterations that have resulted from natural forces (see Backus, this volume), while the recent biodiversity losses have been attributed primarily to human activity. Most of the human-induced impacts are encompassed by one of the following six categories: 1) habitat loss and degradation, 2) introduced invasive species, 3) environmental pollution, 4) disease and parasitism, 5) unsustainable use of some species, and 6) global climate change (Gibbons and Stangel 1999). An additional category includes declines or extinctions that are unexplained because of a lack of historical data on species or the absence of concurrent environmental data. Of course, declines in biodiversity occur in some regions as a consequence of natural forces and factors that are always in operation. All research ecologists would agree also that some recognizable losses of biodiversity may be the result of the cumulative effect or interaction of more than one of the previously listed potential causes (Gibbons et al. 2000).

Scientific Concepts

As with any scientific topic of investigation with global impact, concepts and paradigms are based on an accumulation of the ideas, perspectives, discoveries, and opinions of numerous people. The issues associated with biodiversity range from the basic definitions of the term itself to the identification of the primary factors that influence species numbers and patterns of abundance.

Many of the early discussions of biological diversity focused on biodiversity in its broadest sense, referring to **natural variability** that can include genetic makeup within an organism or species, **morphological** features within species, or ecological attributes of regional plant/animal communities (Williams et al. 1994; Wilson 1992). In most situations, however, the taxonomic diversity of species (**species richness**) and the abundance of individuals of each species present in a prescribed area (**species evenness**) serve as practical indicators of biodiversity that can be measured by ecologists and understood by the general public. Using species richness (the total number of species present in a given area) as a basic measure of biodiversity, a variety of concepts that are fundamental to present-day views among ecologists become apparent.

ISLAND BIOGEOGRAPHY

An early revelation about species diversity was that the number of species associated with a prescribed land area was dependent on both the size of suitable habitat and its distance from other land areas from which colonization might occur (for background information, see MacArthur and Wilson 1967). Although a variety of subtle concepts and ramifications were proposed and mathematical expressions of relationships were made, the basic formula was simple: Large islands, which are more likely to have a higher diversity of habitats and **ecological niches,** and islands close to others or to the mainland, which allow a higher rate of colonization, are likely to have higher biodiversity than smaller ones or ones that are more isolated (**species–area relationship**).

An aspect of **island biogeography** that is pertinent in a consideration of biodiversity in modern times is that isolated islands are more likely to have evolved a fauna that is defenseless against invasions by new predators or competitors. This concept is particularly noteworthy in regard to the extinctions of such species as the dodo from the island of Mauritius; the elimination of several species of giant, flightless moas of New Zealand; and the extirpation of giant tortoises from many of the Galapagos Islands. The demise of each of these species came about as a consequence of human exploration and colonization, which included overhunting by humans and the intentional or accidental introduction of domestic animals and rats. Presumably, islands more closely associated with the mainland and characterized by frequent colonization and recolonization by a variety of species would have evolved a different and more varied faunal and floral array and been less susceptible to the early visitations by humans. Although modern-day agricultural, industrial, and urban impacts would arguably have reduced fauna and flora both on islands and on the mainland anyway, the earliest losses of biodiversity as a result of human colonization around the world came long before environmental concerns were being expressed by scientists.

An extension of the theory of island biogeography that is pertinent to current ecological concerns is that fragmentation of natural habitats (for example, as a result of highway systems, agriculture, or development) is damaging to biodiversity within many ecosystems. The island biogeography concept is applicable in these situations as well because **habitat fragmentation** is, in essence, creating "islands" of habitat that are separated from each other in a variety of ways. For example, an interstate highway or other large, busy roadway through a forest virtually divides the habitat into two separately functioning, smaller units in which nonflying species are afforded only limited opportunity for migratory exchange. Thus, biodiversity among some taxonomic groups will be more likely to decline as the availability of suitable habitat is reduced in size and becomes isolated from similar habitat (see Haskell, this volume).

A common conservation strategy employed by ecologists to counteract the effects of habitat fragmentation and destruction is the designation of terrestrial, freshwater aquatic, and marine **ecological reserves** to help stem the loss of biodiversity. Establishing reserves in areas of suitable habitat at a regional scale is viewed by many as a concept that can effectively allow for the persistence of at least some natural assemblages of plants and animals. Ecological reserves ideally encompass entire ecosystems, such that all native species in a particular type of ecosystem are protected from human impacts. **Wildlife refuges** of the U.S. Fish and Wildlife Service, military bases, and national parks in the United States and other countries have all been used as examples of protected systems where native species can flourish. However, although most wildlife reserves and refuges are established officially on government-controlled public lands, private lands usually harbor most of the species of a region in the United States because in most parts of the country, especially in the eastern states, private lands constitute a greater acreage of undeveloped habitat than do public lands. For example, in Alabama, approximately 5% (1,875 square miles) of total forest habitat is in public ownership compared to the remaining 33,906 square miles controlled by the forest products industry, corporations, and nonindustrial private owners (Hartsell and Brown 2002). As a result, habitat protection by private landowners can contribute greatly to maintaining regional biodiversity. In addition, although the concept of protecting public lands is applied worldwide as a conservation tool against human-caused impacts to natural systems, the protective laws and regulations necessary on public lands are not always enforced. For example, turtle conservationists have come to recognize that one cause of the rapid decline and disappearance of tortoise and freshwater turtle populations in Asia (Buhlmann et al. 2002) is the ineffectiveness of enforcement and protection within so-called protected areas in many countries of the world. Although having effective enforcement is a goal in the long run, species will go extinct in the short term if we wait and rely on enforcement measures to work.

ECOSYSTEMS AND BIODIVERSITY

Ecosystems are extraordinarily complex; they are not simply assemblages of different species of living things but also include those physical and chemical characteristics of the environment that act on the organisms. It is the combination of biotic factors, such as competition with individuals for food, mates, and space, and the potential dangers of predation, along with abiotic factors, such as climate and water availability, that determines the diversity of species and the abundance of individuals that will be found in a particular ecosystem. Some species may be widespread, occupying a variety of ecosystems in different geographic regions, while others are **endemic**, confined to a particular geographic region. The number of endemic species in a particular area is a useful measure of biodiversity: The greater the number of endemic species, the greater the importance of an ecosystem from an ecologist's perspective. If an endemic species is driven to extinction, there are no additional geographic areas in which it exists. This idea has resulted in the identification of **biodiversity hot spots**, which are particular regions that are notable for their high level of biodiversity and the high number of rare and endemic species present (see figure 2.1). Twenty-five global biodiversity hot spots have been identified by the organization Conservation International, most of them in the tropics (Brooks et al. 2002; Myers et al. 2000).

Although a popular focus of attention on habitat loss is in biodiversity hot spots or in tropical regions of the world, the temperate zones are also under formidable assault on every continent, including in highly developed and presumably environmentally enlightened countries. For example, more than 80% of the acreage of historical wetlands has been destroyed in certain parts of North America, and in the southeastern United States, only 3% of the longleaf pine habitat remains intact (Gibbons et al. 2000). An assumption that can be made is that the destruction of such crucial habitats has led to losses of populations of native species, both plants and animals, and is directly responsible for the official recognition of some as threatened, endangered, or extinct.

HUMAN IMPACTS

Human alteration of the environment has had and will continue to have tremendous impacts on biodiversity. On the basis of a variety of scientific data, it is now reasonable to conclude that these impacts are contributing to an extinction event comparable to the five previous mass extinctions recorded in geological history (see Backus, this volume).

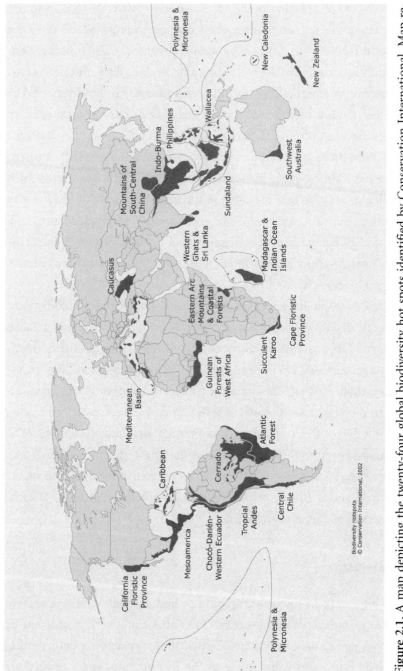
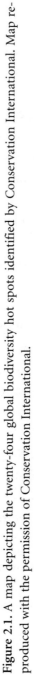

Figure 2.1. A map depicting the twenty-four global biodiversity hot spots identified by Conservation International. Map reproduced with the permission of Conservation International.

The booming human population, combined with the resulting high levels of land use change and consumption of natural resources, is considered by many to be the single most important factor affecting today's biodiversity, both in particular regions and on a global scale. There are currently approximately 6.2 billion people who are dependent on resources and ecosystem services provided by the earth. This number is expected to increase to 11 billion by the last half of the 21st century before leveling off; as this number increases, so will our reliance on the products of our environment. In most situations, as a region becomes overpopulated, human quality of life declines because of a loss of space and exhaustion of natural resources. When this happens, wildlife species also lose places to live and food to eat, resulting in further decline in environmental quality. The issue is exceedingly complex and provocative, but in the view of many ecologists today, virtually all our major environmental problems, including the loss of biodiversity, owe their origin to severe human overpopulation on a global scale.

On a somewhat positive note, while the human population is continuing to increase, the rate of increase is slowing; statistics show that the world's population increased by 64% between 1950 and 1975 and by 48% between 1975 and 2000. This trend, though slightly comforting to many, still does not bode well for biological diversity. An increase of almost 5 billion people requires more housing, more food, and more natural resources and results in the production of more wastes that need to be stored somewhere. The area and resources needed to support the additional members of the flourishing human population will surely affect the diversity of other organisms as a result of activities that can be classified into the six categories previously mentioned: 1) habitat loss and degradation, 2) introduced invasive species, 3) environmental pollution, 4) disease and parasitism, 5) unsustainable use of some species, and 6) global climate change (Gibbons and Stangel 1999).

1. *Habitat loss and degradation.* Virtually every ecologist familiar with native species in any major group of plants or animals would agree

that biodiversity is declining throughout the world as a consequence of the fragmentation, loss, and degradation of natural habitats. Land use change, including urban development, highway construction, and permanent deforestation, deals serious blows to species diversity across the world on a daily basis as a consequence of habitat fragmentation, wetland losses, and other landscape-level problems (Vos and Opdam 1993). For example, loss or degradation of suitable habitat has been documented to be the largest single factor contributing to declines of **amphibians** and reptiles on a worldwide scale (Alford and Richards 1999; Gibbons et al. 2000; Semlitsch and Bodie 1998). Therefore, extinction rates are considered by many ecologists to be at an all-time high because of habitat loss. Current extinction rates have been estimated to be thousands of times higher than **background extinction** rates (see Backus, this volume; Powledge 1998; Tuxill and Bright 1998).

2. *Introduced invasive species.* The introduction of invasive species, also referred to as "exotic species," can have devastating effects on those species that are native to a particular area. The displacement or extinction of native species as a result of introduced species is considered to be one of the most serious of the current threats to the biodiversity of natural ecosystems. Species have been observed to invade previously uninhabited areas naturally, for example, when land bridges become established between two previously unlinked geographic areas; however, as humans have become more adept at global travel and colonization, the invasion of exotic species has increased dramatically. In some cases, invasive species have been documented to outcompete or prey on native species, driving them to extinction. The zebra mussel (*Dreissena polymorpha*), a Caspian Sea native that was accidentally introduced into the Great Lakes when ballast water from ships was dumped in the mid-1980s, now inhabits all the Great Lakes and many river systems and lakes in the eastern United States. This species has caused myriad problems, including the clogging of intake valves and water pipes and competition with native species,

leading to the dramatic decline in the number of native freshwater mussels in the Great Lakes and other eastern waterways (Ricciardi et al. 1998; Schloesser and Nalepa 1994).

3. *Environmental pollution.* Of the various human-induced environmental impacts on biodiversity, the degradation of habitats and loss of species populations as a consequence of environmental pollution became perhaps the first to be broadly recognized and accepted as a problem by both scientists and the general public. Among the factors influencing public attitudes that environmental pollution was an environmental hazard that needed to be controlled was the success of the book *Silent Spring,* published in 1962 by Rachel Carson. The book brought attention to the devastation of birds and other wildlife resulting from unregulated pesticides (particularly DDT) and other forms of environmental pollution. Additional scientific studies documenting pollution of the air, water, and land from a variety of industrial, agricultural, and urban sources provided unequivocal evidence and examples of losses in local and regional biodiversity.

4. *Disease and parasitism.* Disease and parasitism have always been recognized as debilitating to individuals of many species of plants and animals. According to Daszak et al. (2000), some infectious wildlife diseases "pose a substantial threat to the conservation of global biodiversity." Diseases that potentially can have substantial impacts on wildlife species have three basic origins: 1) contagion from domestic animals, 2) human interference with the natural environment (such as introduced blights, parasites, or contagious diseases), and 3) natural occurrences within wildlife populations (Daszak et al. 2000). Each of these, or often a combination of two or all three, has led to numerous wildlife disease epidemics or pandemics that have resulted in a loss of biodiversity, even from more than a century ago. For example, in the late 1800s, a virus that affects hoofed animals was introduced into Africa from Asia. Within a few years, 9% of the buffalo populations in Kenya had been eliminated. Secondary effects on regional biodiversity resulted because of the biological dependence

other animals had on buffalo. Thus, predator populations declined in numbers, and populations of one species, the tsetse fly, became locally extinct (Daszak et al. 2000). Diseases continue to be major threats to the diversity of all taxonomic groups in all habitats and regions of the world.

5. *Unsustainable use of some species.* Unsustainable use of a species occurs when overexploitation results in situations in which a species cannot replace its numbers at the rate at which they are being removed from the habitat. A loss in biodiversity due to the decline in or elimination of a single species or closely related taxonomic group of species can result as a consequence of commercial overharvesting that is unsustainable. One of the most dramatic examples of unsustainable use at the beginning of the 21st century was identified as the Asian turtle crisis. Of the approximately 300 species of freshwater turtles and terrestrial tortoises in the world, Asia has a greater number of species than the other continents. Of these Asian turtles, 75% are ranked as endangered or vulnerable by conservation biologists (Buhlmann et al. 2002), with the primary problems in most countries being unregulated commercial trade that leads to unsustainable removal of turtles and tortoises from the wild.

6. *Global climate change.* A change in the earth's climate due to increases in the concentrations of atmospheric greenhouse gases, including carbon dioxide (CO_2), has been linked to changes in the diversity of some species. These changes may be categorized as one of four types of change: 1) changes in species abundance in certain areas or changes in species distribution as organisms migrate to areas with temperatures that are physiologically tolerable; 2) changes in the timing of biological phenomena, including breeding, migration, flowering, or egg production; 3) changes in the morphology of organisms, including sex ratio (Janzen 1994) and body size (Post et al. 1999); and 4) changes in genetic frequencies of particular alleles (Root et al. 2003). Changes included in any one of the four categories could have lasting effects on biodiversity at any one of the three lev-

els previously discussed: ecosystems, species, or genetic. The Monte Verde golden toad (*Bufo periglenes*), a species endemic to the cloud forests of Costa Rica, experienced abrupt extinction in the late 1980s. This event has been attributed to unusually warm and dry conditions in the misty cloud forests that resulted in the decline in the numbers and disappearances of 20 other frog species from the Monte Verde cloud forests at around the same time (Pounds et al. 1999).

Indicators of a Current Biodiversity Crisis: The IUCN Red List

If one consults the current literature on biodiversity, it becomes apparent that extinction rates are considered by many ecologists to be at an all-time high and that we may be in the midst of a sixth mass extinction event, accelerated by the effects of human impacts on our environment (see Backus, this volume). Information about the conservation status of a wide range of species is available online through the World Conservation Union, formerly known as the International Union for Conservation of Nature and Natural Resources (IUCN). This information is summarized and regularly updated in the Red List of Threatened Species at http://redlist.org (IUCN 2002). To be listed on the IUCN Red List, species must be classified under one of the two extinct categories (extinct or extinct in the wild) or one of the four threatened categories (critically endangered, endangered, vulnerable, or near threatened) and must therefore meet at least one of the criteria used to delineate these categories. These criteria include 1) drastic reduction in the size of a population over the past 10 years or three generations, 2) reduction in the geographic range over which a particular species has been recorded, 3) reduction in the size of a population, and 4) increased probability of extinction in the wild (IUCN 2002).

Inclusion on the Red List does not necessarily indicate that a species will face immediate extinction, but it is an indicator that a species faces an increased risk of extinction in the future. Some species have been the target of intensive conservation and management efforts and have even been delisted, such as the Lord Howe Island stick insect and the Bavarian pine vole, which were believed to be extinct and included on the 2000 Red List and then delisted on their rediscovery prior to the publication of the 2002 Red List. Although the Red List can be considered the most comprehensive listing of threatened and extinct organisms available at this time, it may still be considered an underestimate of the actual number of species at risk of extinction. The reason for this is that while mammals, birds, reptiles, amphibians, and fishes are relatively well studied, many species of invertebrates and plants are not as well known, and many species even remain unknown to science. Add this to the fact that the Red List does not take into consideration species of fungi, protista, or bacteria that might be threatened or extinct, and it is logical to conclude that the list is not a comprehensive count and is in fact an underestimate of the number of species at risk.

What becomes apparent when examining the statistics published by the IUCN is that the rate of extinction that we now see is far beyond the estimated natural rate of extinction, considered to be one species per million per year (Wilson 2002). The number of plant species included on the 2002 Red List totaled 5,714, up from 5,611 listed in the 2000 version. The number of animal species (both vertebrate and invertebrate) included on the 2002 Red List was 5,453, an increase of 18 species over the number listed in 2000, which included 5,435 species of vertebrates and invertebrates. Although some of the numbers of animal species included on the lists have remained relatively steady since 2000, it should be noted that the numbers of threatened mammal species increased from 1,130 in 2000 to 1,137 in 2002 and that the number of threatened bird species increased from 1,183 in 2000 to 1,192 in 2002. A look at the statistics for total numbers of species threatened within these groups provides an even better idea of the extent of the loss. According to data compiled by the IUCN for the 2002 Red List, approximately one-quarter of the world's mammal species and 12% of the world's bird species are in danger of extinction. For reasons previously discussed, it is difficult to cite similar statistics for other, lesser-studied groups, but the trend is similar. In order for us to be provided with a more complete picture of the status of biodiversity, it will be necessary to increase research in this area through diversity measurement and monitoring techniques that will, in turn, require the participation of more scientists in biodiversity research.

Measuring Biodiversity

Assessing biodiversity in terms of species richness within a habitat, ecosystem, or region should theoretically be a straightforward process: define the boundaries being assessed and count the number of species in that particular area. In practice, measuring biodiversity, especially in regard to changing patterns, is far more difficult than envisioned by the casual observer. Knowledge of special techniques, past environmental conditions, and taxonomic expertise can all be essential elements in enumerating the biodiversity of a defined area.

TECHNIQUES OF INVENTORY AND MONITORING

Techniques used to inventory and monitor population trends at global, regional, or local scales are as varied as the taxonomic groups of interest. For example, the methods used for sampling ants, reptiles, grasses, and mushrooms vary enormously not only among the taxonomic groups but also within them. Additional considerations would have to be made between sampling done in tropical versus temperate regions as well as during different seasons. The fact that there are organismal, regional, and seasonal variations in sampling and monitoring techniques makes the task of measuring and conserving biodiversity more challenging; however, the importance of these efforts in the face of unprecedented habitat loss and resulting species extinctions cannot be understated.

Biodiversity inventories, if they are to provide useful and accurate information, must be undertaken as collaborative efforts. Techniques that have historically been employed in the inventory of biological diversity require a great deal of manpower and are applicable only to relatively small geographic areas. Some of these types of projects involve establishing designated inventory areas that include representatives of all habitat types found within a larger, designated geographic area and identifying the species present in the inventory plots. In Costa Rica, the National Institute for Biodiversity (INBio) was established in 1989 as a result of the efforts of ecologist Dan Janzen and others to conduct an inventory of all the living organisms in Costa Rica.

Large-scale species inventories are currently under way in the United States as the diversity of organisms inhabiting national parks and monuments are under survey as part of a network approach to inventory and monitoring (National Park Service 1995). One example is the Great Smoky Mountains All Taxa Biodiversity Inventory (GSM ATBI). This attempt to identify every species of organism living in the Great Smoky Mountains National Park was first conceived in 1997, officially started in 1999, and continues today. It has been estimated that this monumental undertaking will require 10 to 15 years to complete and will involve a small army of scientists and volunteers working together. A website is maintained by organizers at www.discoverlife.org to provide updates on the status of the inventory.

USING HISTORICAL DATA

Among the most valuable data for estimating rates or magnitude of biodiversity loss are historical records of the abundance and diversity of species (Ponder et al. 2001). While biodiversity inventories are invaluable for providing snapshots regarding the status of biodiversity in particular areas at particular times, historical records are necessary to determine whether variations in populations may be the results of regular cyclical fluctuations or due to permanent losses that might lead to local extirpation or extinction. For example, during the 1980s, amphibian populations were rightfully noted to be declining in many regions of North America (and the rest of the world) from a variety of known and undetermined causes. Overstated claims were made by otherwise respected scientists and environmentalists implying that amphibians were more seriously threatened ecologically than other groups of organisms, such as reptiles and mammals. The undocumented assertions about amphibians were skeptically addressed by other scientists (Beebee 1992; Gibbons et al. 2000; Hedges 1993), but the use of historical data was necessary for fully understanding species declines.

Pechmann and Wilbur (1994) critically reviewed much of the literature on reported amphibian declines. They noted that in most instances, because of natural year-to-year fluctuations in amphibian populations, conclusive documentation of some perceived declines would require long-term surveys of abundance and diversity of an amphibian community in a particular region or habitat. Changes in population size of an amphibian species could easily be misinterpreted as a response to an apparent environmental impact when, in fact, the change might actually be attributed to natural variability if long-term historical data were available for analysis (see Pechmann et al. 1991) or if local reference populations were used as controls.

Evidence now exists to support the position that amphibian numbers are clearly declining and that amphibian biodiversity is imperiled throughout the world (Houlahan et al. 2000). Nonetheless, the principle that losses of biodiversity should be interpreted circumspectly by guarding against overstatement or embellishment is a general one, applicable not only to amphibians but also to any taxonomic group and warrants a call for careful and credible documentation in specific instances. The availability of reliable historical records can sometimes be a major determinant when making a case that biodiversity has decreased, increased, or remained relatively stable in a particular situation. Research ecologists must be judicious in their use of findings to support an assessment that the distribution and abundance of one or more species have changed or remained the same. A solid foundation of research facts is critical for building a credible case in all declarations of biodiversity loss.

The studies on representatives of all major classes of vertebrates by Cody and Smallwood (1996) are ideal examples of 16 long-term studies that should be continued because of the extensive baseline information they provide for comparisons with other populations and regions as well as for quantifying fluctuations in the same populations over time. Among the longest continual studies of vertebrates in the United States are those by the Savannah River Ecology Laboratory (SREL) in which more than a million captures and observations have been recorded for 100 species of native reptiles and amphibians since 1951 (Gibbons et al. 1997). The SREL records of long-term patterns of distribution and abundance of a region have been used in evaluating a variety of environmental issues of importance at national as well as regional scales (Burke and Gibbons 1995; Pechmann et al. 1991; Semlitsch and Bodie 1998).

TAXONOMIC EXPERTISE

Among the essential components for understanding biodiversity patterns on both regional and global scales are taxonomic experts for various organismal groups. Trained ecologists who know how to collect and identify the species in a target group are necessary to ensure proper sampling and analysis of species data. In some cases, only a handful of scientists trained in the identification of particular types of organisms are available. For example, taxonomic experts are rare not only for species of bacteria, fungi, and some microscopic invertebrates, such as rotifers and tardigrades, but also for many animal groups, including some insects, spiders, and mollusks. Meanwhile, hundreds of individuals are available with the taxonomic skills necessary to provide accurate identifications for groups such as birds, mammals, and trees. Thus, while it may be possible to get accurate identifications for many of the organisms collected during biodiversity inventories, it may be difficult or even impossible to find taxonomic experts for some of the rare specimens that belong to understudied groups, resulting in an incomplete picture of the diversity of a particular area.

Where Is Biodiversity Research Heading?

In predicting the future of research on biodiversity as well as the ultimate future of biodiversity in various regions of the world, the simplest approach is to consider the perspectives of those who study biodiversity and those who influence it. When viewed as an extension of understanding the distribution and abundance of organisms, it is clear that interest in biodiversity has been a central theme among ecologists and evolutionary biologists (even Darwin himself) for well over a century. Presumably, similar interests in biodiversity will prevail in future investigations of natural systems throughout the world. Scientists will continue to focus on issues and questions that center on biodiversity. Included among the conservation considerations will be questions related to how to develop more rapid methods of biodiversity assessment through predictive models, the use of indicator species, or other approaches; how to effectively implement **assurance colonies** of imperiled species on a global scale; and how to prioritize research on biodiversity with regard to taxonomic groups and particular ecosystems.

Meanwhile, people are the ultimate controllers of how much biodiversity will persist in different regions, and most people are captivated by wild things, marvel at species diversity, and are appreciative of natural habitats (Kellert and Wilson 1993). Yet people make trade-offs against the cultural, religious, and socioeconomic influences on their lives that may or may not be conducive to maintaining natural biodiversity. One means of countering the impacts of such trade-offs and of bringing public pressure to bear on stemming the loss of biological diversity is through education that involves familiarizing as many people as possible with the wonders of the natural world. People who have been introduced to the diversity of living things on local, regional, and global scales can be expected to become strong advocates for maintaining natural levels of biological diversity because of the tangible and intangible benefits that accrue to the human species.

Acknowledgments

Manuscript preparation was aided by Financial Assistance Award Number DE-FC09-96SR18546 from the U.S. Department of Energy to the University of Georgia Research Foundation and the Savannah River Ecology Laboratory.

REFERENCES

Agosti, D., J. D. Majer, L. E. Alonso, and T. R. Schultz. 2000. *Ants: Standard methods for measuring and monitoring biodiversity.* Biological Diversity Handbook Series. Washington, D.C.: Smithsonian Institution Press.

Alford, R.A., and S. J. Richards. 1999. Global amphibian declines: A problem in applied ecology. *Annual Review of Ecology and Systematics* 30:133–65.

Andrewartha, H. G., and L. C. Birch. 1954. *The distribution and abundance of animals.* Chicago: University of Chicago Press.

Beebee, T. J. C. 1992. Amphibian decline? *Nature* 355(6356):120.

Brooks, T. M., R. A. Mittermeier, C. G. Mittermeier, G. A. B. da Fonseco, A. B. Rylands, W. R. Konstant, P. Flick, J. Pilgrim, S. Oldfield, G. Magin, and C. Hilton-Taylor. 2002. Habitat loss and extinction in the hotspots of biodiversity. *Conservation Biology* 16(4):909–23.

Buhlmann, K. A., R. Hudson, and A. J. Rhodin. 2002. *Turtle Conservation Fund. A global action plan for conservation of tortoises and freshwater turtles.* Washington, D.C.: Conservation International and Chelonian Research Foundation.

Burke, V. J., and J. W. Gibbons. 1995. Terrestrial buffer zones and wetland conservation: A case study of freshwater turtles in a Carolina bay. *Conservation Biology* 9:1365–69.

Bush, M. B. 2000. *Ecology of a changing planet.* 2nd ed. Upper Saddle River, N.J.: Prentice Hall.

Cody, Martin L., and Jeffrey A. Smallwood, eds. 1996. *Long-term studies of vertebrate communities.* San Diego: Academic.

Daszak, P., A. A. Cunningham, and A. D. Hyatt. 2000. Emerging infectious diseases of wildlife—Threats to biodiversity and human health. *Science* 287:443–49.

Dobson, A. P. 1998. *Conservation and biodiversity.* New York: Freeman.

Donahue, D. L. 2000. *The Western Range revisited: Removing livestock from public lands to conserve native biodiversity.* Legal History of North America Series, vol. 5. Norman: University of Oklahoma Press.

Gibbons, W., and A. R. Gibbons. 1998. *Ecoviews: Snakes, snails, and environmental tales.* Tuscaloosa: University of Alabama Press.

Gibbons, J. W., D. E. Scott, T. Ryan, K. Buhlmann, T. Tuberville, J. Greene, T. Mills, Y. Leiden, S. Poppy, C. Winne, and B. Metts. 2000. The global decline of reptiles, déjà vu amphibians. *BioScience* 50:653–66.

Gibbons, J. W., and P. W. Stangel. 1999. *Proceedings of the Partners in Amphibian and Reptile Conservation (PARC) Conference.* Herp Outreach Publication, no. 2. Aiken, S.C.: Savannah River Ecology Laboratory.

Gibbons, J. W., et al. 1997. Perceptions of species abundance, distribution, and diversity: Lessons from four decades of sampling on a government-managed reserve. *Environmental Management* 21(2):259–68.

Gore, A. 1992. *Earth in the balance.* Boston: Houghton Mifflin.

Hallac, D. E., and J. E. Marsden. 2001. Comparison of conservation strategies for unionids threatened by zebra mussels (*Dreissena polymorpha*): Periodic cleaning vs. quarantine and translocation. *Journal of the North American Benthological Society* 20(2):200–10.

Hartsell, A. J., and M. A. Brown. 2002. *Forest statistics of Alabama, 2000.* USDA Forest Service Research Bulletin SRS-67. Asheville, N.C.: USDA Department of Agriculture, Forest Service, Southern Research Station.

Hedges, S. Blair. 1993. Global amphibian declines: A perspective from the Caribbean. *Biodiversity and Conservation* 2:290–303.

Horton, D. R., E. R. Miliczky, D. A. Broers, R. R. Lewis, and C. O. Calkins. 2001. Numbers, diversity, and phenology of spiders (Araneae) overwintering in cardboard bands placed in pear and apple orchards of central Washington. *Annals of the Entomological Society of America* 94(3):405–14.

Houlahan, J. E., C. S. Findlay, B. R. Schmidt, A. H. Meyer, and S. L. Kuzmin. 2000. Quantitative evidence for global amphibian population declines. *Nature* 404(6779):752–55.

Hubbell, S. P. 2001. *The unified neutral theory of biodiversity and biogeography.* Monographs in Population Biology, no. 32. Princeton, N.J.: Princeton University Press.

Hunter, M. L. 1999. *Maintaining biodiversity in forest ecosystems.* Cambridge, Mass.: Cambridge University Press.

International Union for Conservation of Nature and Natural Resources–World Conservation Union. 2002. The IUCN Red List of Threatened Species. http://redlist.org.

Janzen, F. J. 1994. Climate change and temperature-dependent sex determination in reptiles. *Proceedings of the National Academy of Sciences* 91(16):7487–90.

Kellert, S. R., and E. O. Wilson, eds. 1993. The biophilia hypothesis. Washington, D.C.: Island Press.

MacArthur, R., and E. O. Wilson. 1967. *The theory of island biogeography.* Princeton, N.J.: Princeton University Press.

Myers, N., R. A. Mittermeier, C. G. Mittermeier, G. A. B. da Fonseca, and J. Kent. 2000. Biodiversity hotspots for conservation priorities. *Nature* 403(6772):853–58.

National Park Service. 1995. *Natural resource inventory and monitoring guideline.* NPS-75. Washington, D.C.: National Park Service.

Noss, R. F. 2001. Beyond Kyoto: Forest management in a time of rapid climate change. *Conservation Biology* 15(3):578–90.

Novacek, M. J. 2001. *The biodiversity crisis: Losing what counts.* American Museum of Natural History Books. New York: The New Press.

Odum, E. P. 1971. *Fundamentals of ecology.* 3rd ed. Philadelphia: Saunders.

Pechmann, J. H. K., D. E. Scott, R. D. Semlitsch, J. P. Caldwell, L. J. Vitt, and J. W. Gibbons. 1991. Declining amphibian populations: The problem of separating human impacts from natural fluctuations. *Science* 253:892–95.

Pechmann, J. H. K., and H. M. Wilbur. 1994. Putting declining amphibian populations in perspective: Natural fluctuations and human impacts. *Herpetologica* 50:65–84.

Pimm, S. L. 2001. *The world according to Pimm: A scientist audits the Earth.* New York: McGraw-Hill.

Ponder, W. F., G. A. Carter, P. Flemons, and R. R. Chapman. 2001. Evaluation of museum collection data for use in biodiversity assessment. *Conservation Biology* 15(3):648–57.

Post, E., R. Langvatn, M. C. Forchhammer, and N. C. Stenseth. 1999. Environmental variation shapes sexual dimorphism in red deer. *Proceedings of the National Academy of Sciences* 96:4467–71.

Pounds, J. A., M. P. L. Fogden, and J. H. Campbell. 1999. Biological responses to climate change on a tropical mountain. *Nature* 398(6728):611–15.

Powledge, F. 1998. Biodiversity at the crossroads. *BioScience* 48:347–52.

Ricciardi, A., R. J. Neves, and J. B. Rasmussen. 1998. Impending extinction of North American freshwater mussels (Unionida) following the zebra mussel (*Dreissena polymorpha*) invasion. *Journal of Animal Ecology* 67:613–19.

Root, T. L., J. T. Price, K. R. Hall, S. H. Schneider, C. Rosenzweig, and J. A. Pounds. 2003. Fingerprints of global warming on wild animals and plants. *Nature* 421(6918):57–60.

Schloesser, D. W., and T. F. Nalepa. 1994. Dramatic decline of native unionid bivalves in offshore waters of western Lake Erie after infestation by the zebra mussel, *Dreissena polymorpha*. *Canadian Journal of Fisheries and Aquatic Sciences* 51:2234–42.

Semlitsch, R. D. 2000. Size does matter: The value of small isolated wetlands. *Environmental Law Institute*, January–February, 5–6, 13.

Semlitsch R. D., and J. R. Bodie. 1998. Are small, isolated wetlands expendable? *Conservation Biology* 12:1129–33.

Smith, C. H. 2000. *Biodiversity studies*. Lanham, Md.: Scarecrow Press.

Tuxill, J., and C. Bright. 1998. Losing strands in the web of life. In *State of the World*. Edited by L. Brown, C. Flavin, and H. French. New York: Norton, 41–58.

Vos, Claire C., and Paul Opdam, eds. 1993. *Landscape ecology of a stressed environment*. New York: Chapman & Hall.

Wall, D., H. Mooney, G. Adams, G. Boxshall, A. Dobson, T. Nakashizuka, J. Seyani, C. Samper, and J. Sarukhán. 2001. An international biodiversity observation year. *Trends in Ecology and Evolution* 16(1):52–54.

Ward, J. V., and K. Tockner. 2001. Biodiversity: Towards a unifying theme for river ecology. *Freshwater Biology* 46:807–19.

Williams, P. H., K. J. Gaston, and C. J. Humphries. 1994. Do conservationists and molecular biologists value differences between organisms in the same way? *Biodiversity Letters* 2:67–78.

Wilson, E. O. 1992. *The diversity of life*. Cambridge, Mass.: Harvard University Press.

———. 2002. *The future of life*. New York: Knopf.

SUGGESTED READINGS

Crist, E. 2002. Quantifying the biodiversity crisis. *Wild Earth* 12(1):16–19.

Gibbs, W. W. 2001. On the termination of species. *Scientific American* 85(5):40–49.

Novacek, M. J. 2001. *The biodiversity crisis: Losing what counts.* American Museum of Natural History Books. New York: New Press.

Pimm, S. L. 2001. *The world according to Pimm: A scientist audits the Earth.* New York: McGraw-Hill.

Wilson, E. O. 1988. *Biodiversity.* Washington, D.C.: National Academy Press.

———. 1992. *The diversity of life.* Cambridge, Mass.: Harvard University Press.

3

Diminishing Songbirds

CONSERVATION
BIOLOGY CASE
STUDY OF
EASTERN
SONGBIRDS

David G. Haskell

This chapter illustrates the general principles of conservation biology through a case study of songbird conservation in the eastern United States. The case study approach is helpful for two reasons. First, because conservation biology is an applied science that aims to manage and preserve biodiversity, the field cannot be understood apart from real organisms in real landscapes. Second, successful conservation relies on the insights of many different disciplines. This synergy is best illustrated by weaving the various disciplinary strands around one issue.

The structure of the chapter is as follows. First, the relevant natural history of songbirds is outlined. Then the fundamental conservation issues involving these animals is described. Finally some of the ethical, political, and economic challenges of conserving songbirds are introduced. Along the way, the general issues and themes that recur throughout the science of conservation biology are highlighted.

Why use songbirds as a case study? Certainly not because birds are a representative sample of all of life's diversity; birds are large, **endothermic** vertebrates, whereas most animals are small **invertebrates**. Just 3% of animals are vertebrates (at most, as many invertebrate species have yet to be described), and only 20% of vertebrates are birds. Why, then, focus on birds? There are two answers to this question. One is primarily esthetic, and the other is more scientific. First, birds appeal to humans. They use the same modes of communication as we do (visual and acoustic displays), whereas most other organisms communicate using modalities that are more hidden to us (odors and even electrical fields). Birds are also on the same scale as humans; they are active primarily during the daylight hours, and they live in many of the same habitats. Birds are therefore the most obvious and beautiful organisms in many ecosystems. The second argument in favor of using birds as a biodiversity case study stems from their accessibility: We know a great deal about these animals. Whole scientific societies and journals are devoted to the study of this one taxon. Both professional biologists and amateur birdwatchers have spent hours in the field documenting the distribution and abundance of birds, especially in the past 50 years. Because birds are relatively well known, they provide us with a window into the causes and consequences of population declines that are not always available for other organisms. Birds may also serve as readily observed **bioindicators** of more general problems in ecosystems. This role as indicators has been dubbed the "canary in the coal mine effect." Miners once carried caged canaries deep into coal mines because the canaries were more sensitive to carbon monoxide poisoning than were the coal miners. If the canary keeled over, the coal miners knew that they needed to evacuate—bad luck for the canary but very useful for the miners. Likewise, many have argued that population declines of birds indicate that whole **ecosystems** may be in trouble. Thus, songbirds illustrate the first general theme from the science of conservation biology: that conspicuous, popular, or easy-to-monitor species are often used as indicators or surrogates for the rest of the biota (Pearson and Carroll 1998; Price and Rotenberry 2000; Uliczka and Angelstam 2000). The success of this approach, however, depends on the assumption that most species within an ecosystem show similar responses to habitat changes. This is a sound assumption in simple cases (for example, paving over a forest will eliminate all forest inhabitants) but may need testing in more complex situations (for example, converting a uniform forest into a patchwork of pasture and forest may harm some species but benefit others).

An Overview of the Natural History of the Songbirds of Eastern North America

About half of all the birds in eastern North America are songbirds (order: Passeriformes). Flycatchers, swallows, crows, thrushes, chickadees, warblers, vireos, sparrows, finches, and wrens are some of the more common songbirds in eastern North America. These birds are remarkably diverse. Most songbirds feed on high-energy foods, such as insects, seeds, or small fruits, and many songbirds migrate. Migration is a complex process, but for the sake of simplicity most songbirds can be divided into three categories: **long-distance migrants, short-distance migrants**, and **nonmigratory**. Most long-distance migrants belong to bird families that evolved and still have most of their diversity in the tropics. Thus, the warblers, vireos, and tanagers that come to North America every summer are tropical birds making a brief foray into the temperate zone to take advantage of a seasonal explosion of food resources. Some of these long-distance migrants pull off incredible feats of endurance. For example, blackpoll warblers fly every fall all the way from the coast of New England to the coast of northern South America. This journey over 3,500 kilometers of ocean takes more than 80 hours of nonstop flying. Other songbirds migrate just as far but do most of their traveling over land.

Short-distance migrants abandon the northern limits of their range in winter and move the southern limit of their range southward. Thus, Canadian bird-watchers see American robins only in the summer, Floridian bird-watchers see robins only in the winter, and Tennesseean bird-watchers see them all year. Nonmigratory species, such as chickadees, do not migrate, and many spend most of their lives in one patch of forest.

Songbirds breed by pairing up and defending territories (some species also defend winter territories). These territories provide food for the nesting pair and for the nestlings, and territorial defense helps reduce (but not eliminate) **cuckoldry**. Songbirds build nests in tree cavities (chickadees and nuthatches), high in the branches of trees (orioles and many warblers), in shrubs (many thrushes), or on the ground (some sparrows and warblers). The female generally incubates the eggs, and both sexes feed the young. The parents often continue to feed the young for several weeks after they have left the nest. Some species can raise several **broods** each year; others are restricted to just one (a brood is one nest full of young).

General Questions in Conservation Biology

Just as doctors monitor the vital signs of their patients, conservation biologists monitor the "health" of the organisms they study. Conservation biologists generally first ask questions about general population trends, then move on to more specific questions about the causes of any changes. For example, we might ask whether the abundance of a species has changed through time or whether the species' range has expanded or contracted. Then, we could ask whether there have been any **demographic** changes (such as increased mortality of young birds or decreased reproduction of adults) that might have caused population expansions and contractions. Next, we could study the causes of these demographic changes. Has habitat availability changed, for example? This chapter discusses how biologists monitor the populations of songbirds and then examines the causes of these changes.

Monitoring Populations

Information about long-term trends of songbird populations in eastern North America comes from two primary sources: radar images of flocks of migrating birds and large-scale surveys of birds over most of the continent.

Birds often migrate in large flocks, and these flocks show up on radar images. Comparisons of radar images recorded on the Gulf coast of the United States show that there were 50% fewer large flocks of migrating birds moving over the radar stations in the late 1980s compared to the mid-1960s. These data provide evidence that the overall number of migrant birds has declined sharply over the past few decades. The radar data do not, however, provide information about which species of birds are declining and where these species live (Gauthreaux 1992).

The **Breeding Bird Survey** (BBS) does provide species- and region-level information (Sauer et al. 2000). This survey was started in 1966 and has been conducted every year since. Surveyors all across the United States and Canada drive along standardized routes and stop at regular intervals to note all the birds seen or heard. The strengths of the BBS data lie in the fact that all surveyors use the same methods, the survey covers many years, and the survey encompasses a huge geographic area. Thus, the BBS data are considered one of the best sources of information about breeding bird population trends in North America. Before discussing these trends, however, it is necessary to briefly outline some of the problems with BBS data. These problems are not fatal, but BBS data should always be interpreted in the light of these biases. First, BBS surveys are conducted from roads, so the surveys are not randomized samples of all habitats but rather depend on the routes followed by roads. BBS data will not, therefore, provide much information about bird populations in roadless areas. Second, although skilled observers conduct all BBS surveys, there is variability in how well observers can identify birds. Much of this identification is made using knowledge of birdsongs and calls, and an observer with 20 years of experience (or, better, hearing) is likely to find more birds than is an observer with 10 years of experience. Third, although the BBS has been running for more than 30 years, it cannot capture the full history of bird populations. Much of the bird habitat in North America had already been logged, mined, farmed, or developed by the 1960s, so BBS data will tell us about only recent changes, not longer-term trends.

Keeping these problems in mind, what can we learn from the BBS data? Clearly, some species are declining rapidly. The cerulean warbler declined by an average of 4% per year from 1966 to 1999, and the wood thrush has declined by 1.9% per year. Other species seem to have held steady (the scarlet tanager has shown no significant change from 1966 to 1999), while some species have increased significantly (the cedar waxwing increased by 1.5% per year from 1966 to 1999).

A few general trends emerge from the BBS data. First, more grassland-breeding species have declined than have forest-dwelling birds. More ground-nesting species, species that migrate, and species that nest in open-cup nests have declined than have tree-nesting species, nonmigratory species, and species that nest in cavities. Declines for most species have generally been much more severe in the eastern part of the Midwest than they have on the East Coast. In sum, songbird populations in the United States have been closely monitored for the past 35 years, and in some cases these monitoring efforts have revealed dramatic trends. What might have caused these changes?

Causes of Population Changes

All organisms have physiological, chemical, and behavioral needs that tie them to particular habitats. Thus, a major task for conservation biologists is understanding how changes in habitat translate into changes in populations and hence changes in communities and ecosystems. The next four sections use songbirds to illustrate some of the complexities of this task.

STRUCTURE AND COMPOSITION OF BREEDING HABITAT

The breeding habitat requirements of songbirds are strongly related to vegetation availability. Vegetation can be described in terms of its structure (for example, whether the habitat has a closed canopy of trees, an understory, or open grassy areas) and composition (for example, which species occur in the habitat). Some species have very narrow requirements for both structure and composition (Kirtland's warbler nests only in large tracts of burned jack pine forest). Others are mostly sensitive to structure (black-throated blue warblers nest in forests with a closed canopy and a shrubby understory but are not very sensitive to the type of shrub or tree in which they nest). Other species have extremely broad tastes (American robins will breed in suburbia, shrubby deserts, and eastern woodlands).

When Europeans arrived in North America, the eastern United States was covered by forests interspersed with open areas created by natural disturbances such as wind and fire and by the agricultural activities of Native Americans. The colonists cleared large areas of forest for agriculture, firewood, and towns, and such areas continue to be cleared. This loss of mature forest habitat underlies the decline of some birds. The cerulean warbler mentioned in the previous section nests in the crowns of very large old trees. As these trees have fallen under the ax and the chainsaw, the population of these birds has dwindled rapidly.

Changes in vegetation have, however, benefited some birds in eastern North America. The chestnut-sided warbler, for example, was a very rare bird in the 1800s. This bird breeds in young forests and shrubby areas and over the past 100 years has experienced a population boom as humans have created suitable breeding habitat. Now it is one of the more common breeding warblers in some areas. Other birds breed in grasslands (grasshopper sparrows, golden-winged warblers, bobolinks, and eastern meadowlarks) and have also benefited as humans converted forest to pasture. These birds now present an interesting dilemma for conservationists. In some parts of the East, forests are growing back because land cleared for agriculture is no longer being farmed. As the forests have grown back, many bird species that specialize on old fields and young forests have declined. Thus, these species experienced a boom when the forest was cleared but are now declining as the forest grows back. How should we respond to these population declines? Some argue that we should allow these species to decline. After all, their abundance in the middle of the twentieth century was an artifact of the fact that humans had cleared and then abandoned huge areas of land. Others argue that we should re-create large areas of grassland and scrubby forest for these birds by logging or burning more mature forests.

SPATIAL ARRANGEMENT OF BREEDING HABITAT

Although alterations in the overall acreage of different habitat types constitute a very important cause of changes in the populations of all organisms, these alterations do not tell the whole story. As humans have changed the landscape, they have chopped it into pieces and created a patchwork of different habitats. This **habitat fragmentation** has profound consequences for many species, including birds. To illustrate, consider two simple landscapes (see figure 3.1). Both have half the land covered by forest and half covered by residential housing; they differ only in the spatial arrangement of the two habitats. Landscape A is fragmented into a quilt-like arrangement; landscape B is unfragmented, and each habitat occurs in a uniform block. The consequence of fragmentation is an increase in **edge habitat** (an edge is the intersection between two different habitat types) and a corresponding decrease in **interior habitat** (habitat far from an edge; the exact definition depends on how one defines "far from"). Landscape A has more than eight times as much edge than landscape B; landscape B has a core area removed from the edges, whereas landscape A has no such habitat. Understanding the effects of increases in edge habitat and decreases in interior habitat is therefore an important task for conservation biologists.

Habitat fragmentation has significant consequences for breeding birds. Although some songbirds specialize at breeding on edges (indigo buntings

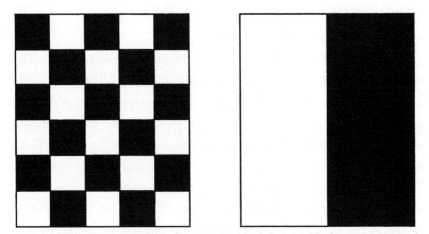

Figure 3.1. Two landscapes. Landscape A, on the left, is highly fragmented. Landscape B, on the right, is unfragmented. Both have the same amount of each habitat type, but landscape B has less edge and more interior habitat.

and eastern towhees), many forest-dwelling species (scarlet tanagers) cannot or will not breed successfully near edges (Rosenberg et al. 1999; Whitcomb et al. 1981). This preference is not an arbitrary whim: Edges have many negative effects for songbirds, and birds that avoid edges may thereby increase their **reproductive success**.

Increased risk of predation on nests is one negative consequence of attempting to breed near edges. Many animals that prey on bird nests (such as raccoons and American crows) are associated with edges, and rates of predation on bird nests are often increased as habitats become more fragmented (Donovan et al. 1995; Robinson et al. 1995; Trine 1998). Fragmentation can also introduce new predators into an area. If housing developments or farms fragment the breeding bird habitat, domestic and feral cats may prey on large numbers of both nestlings and adult birds (Crooks and Soulé 1999; Haskell et al. 2001). By feeding these cats and then letting them roam outside, pet owners are maintaining cat populations at levels that would be unsustainable in nature. Vulnerability to terrestrial nest predators, such as cats, raccoons, and skunks, might explain why more ground-nesting songbird species have declined than have species that nest in trees. Likewise, fewer species that nest in relatively safe tree cavities have declined than have species that nest in unprotected open-cup nests.

Brown-headed cowbirds are also associated with edges, especially those that abut agricultural land (Brittingham and Temple 1983; Coker and Capen 1995). These birds are parasitic: They remove eggs from the nests of other birds, then lay one of their own eggs. Before Europeans colonized North America, cowbirds followed large native mammals, such as bison, on the prairies and were absent or scarce in many parts of the East. When the European colonists cleared large parts of the eastern forest and introduced cattle and horses, the cowbirds moved in. Now many birds that are native to the East are regularly parasitized and will raise the cowbird nestling with their own young. Cowbird parasitism reduces the reproductive output of their hosts, and in some areas cowbirds are so common that nests are parasitized by multiple cowbirds and host parents raise broods composed only of cowbird nestlings. Cowbirds will generally not stray more than a few miles from agricultural land, so their abundance is much lower in unfragmented habitats. Edges also change the food supply for breeding birds. Because edges open forest habitats to wind and sunshine, the leaf litter of the soil is thinned, and there are fewer soil-dwelling insects for breeding birds to feed their nestlings (Burke and Nol 1998; Haskell 2000).

Songbirds therefore illustrate the significance of habitat fragmentation for conservation. Fragmentation breaks up previously continuous habitat and opens the door to nonnative species and edge-adapted predators and parasites and produces changes in **microclimate**.

ALTERATIONS IN MIGRATORY HABITAT

The fact that more species of migrants have declined than have nonmigratory species suggests that factors affecting birds during migration or on the wintering grounds may be an important cause of population declines. Flight is an energetically expensive activity, and migrant birds are dependent on finding food along their long route. For example, blackpoll warblers spend several days on the coast of New England engaging in a gluttonous feast that will produce thick wads of fat under the birds' skin. This fat is the fuel and the source of water for the birds' lengthy migratory journey. Unfortunately for the blackpoll warbler and its fellow migrants, coastal habitats in New England and elsewhere are being converted into housing subdivisions, beach resorts, and other developments that offer birds little food and perhaps increased exposure to predators such as domestic cats. Although the birds spend just a few days of their lives in these "migratory stopover" habitats, changes in these areas can have large impacts on bird populations (Weber and Houston 1997; Weber et al. 1999).

The huge towers that transmit radio, television, and cellular telephone signals present another danger to migrant birds (Bevanger 1994). During bad weather, these towers can kill thousands of birds in one night. The birds seem confused by the "warning" lights on the towers and circle the tower until they collide with the towers' guy wires. We still lack a complete picture of this issue, but the number of radio and cellular telephone towers is increasing rapidly, and some conservationists have claimed that this proliferation presents a significant danger to migrant bird populations.

Finally, it has been suggested that global climate change will change the patterns of prevailing winds over both landmasses and the oceans. Many birds rely on these winds to reduce the costs of migratory flight, and some studies indicate that changes in these winds could make certain migratory routes difficult, with uncertain consequences to the species that use these routes (Sutherland 1998). There is still uncertainty about the effects of climate change on wind patterns, but these changes may have a considerable impact on migrant bird populations.

ALTERATIONS IN WINTERING HABITAT

Migrant songbirds winter in Central and South America, where, just as has happened in North America, native forests are being cleared for timber, housing, industry, and agriculture. These changes have negatively affected some migrant birds. For example, Kentucky warblers winter in native forests and do not thrive in the agricultural fields that are replacing the original forest habitat (Lynch 1992; Robbins et al. 1992). The story is more complex for other migrant songbirds. Black-throated blue warblers, for example, seem to be able to live and feed during the winter in some kinds of agricultural habitats. In general, wintering birds are less vulnerable to changes in habitat than are breeding birds (wintering birds are not affected by changes in populations of nest predators or the availability of nesting sites.) Thus, although some migrant birds may be able to live in agricultural fields in the neotropics, the clearing of native forest may drive the resident breeding birds to extinction.

Coffee plantations provide an interesting example of the interaction between agricultural practices and migrant bird conservation (Greenberg et al. 1997; Moguel and Toledo 1999; Rice and Ward 1996; Sherry 2000). There are two main varieties of coffee: arabica and robusta. Robusta coffee is grown in large **monoculture** plantations, and the coffee beans are processed into products that give us lower-quality coffees, such as instant coffee. Arabica coffee plants provide beans for the premium coffee trade and are grown in either shade or sun plantations. Shade plantations are the more traditional method of coffee production. In these plantations, the coffee plants grow underneath a canopy of native trees. Sun plantations are monocultures of coffee plants growing in rows under the full sun. In the past few decades, many traditional shade plantations have been uprooted and replaced with sun plantations. Grants from the United States Agency for International Development helped foster this transition to sun plantations, which, the agency believed, would offer a better livelihood for farmers. Whether this promise has been fulfilled is open to question; sun plantations require large inputs of costly **agrichemicals** and may deplete the fertility of the soil more rapidly than do shade plantations. Plant species diversity and the structural complexity of the vegetation is much higher in shade plantations than it is in sun plantations. Not surprisingly, bird diversity is also much higher in shade plantations. Indeed, most migrant and resident birds are completely absent from sun coffee plantations. In some areas of Central America where all native forest has been cleared, shade coffee plantations offer the only suitable habitat for many birds. Coffee consumers therefore have a choice between different methods of production, and there is a growing market for shade-grown coffee. It remains to be seen whether this market is strong enough to provide enough economic incentive to slow the large-scale loss of traditional coffee plantations.

This example underscores an important theme in conservation biology: that not all methods of **resource extraction** are equally damaging to biodiversity. Conservation biologists can therefore advise policymakers, the public, and the resource-extracting industries about the most biologically appropriate methods of using our natural environment. Whether this advice is heeded depends on a complex mix of science, policy, economics, and ethics.

Ethical Considerations for Songbird Conservation

Ethical perspectives will determine what our conservation goals should be, and different ethics will produce radically different uses of scientific information. **Anthropocentrism** maintains that we should conserve birds because they provide economic or recreational benefits to humans (see Minteer, this volume). For example, experiments excluding birds from forests have shown that birds eat insect "pests" and therefore reduce damage to trees. This decreased damage may result in higher yields of timber, thus helping human interests. Anthropocentric approaches to conservation tend to emphasize the utility of wildlife. For example, an anthropocentrist might emphasize careful management of fisheries and game animals over the conservation of organisms that, at least superficially, have little economic value. Thus, more government money is spent on turkey and deer management than has ever been spent on nongame songbird conservation. (Hunters also buy hunting licenses and pay a tax on all hunting equipment, so there are more funds available for game animals. Birdwatchers currently pay no such taxes.) An anthropocentrist will also value nongame animals that have utility over those that do not. Thus, areas of the world that have great promise for yielding new drugs derived from animals or plants (such as rain forests) receive more attention from conservationists than do areas that seem to offer less potential (such as deserts).

The very fact that so many humans enjoy watching wildlife also gives birds economic value. The U.S. Fish and Wildlife Service, for example, estimates that in 1996 wildlife watchers generated $29 billion in revenues for motels, restaurants, airlines, and equipment manufacturers in the United States. These expenditures support about 1 million jobs. Many communities have capitalized on this and organize festivals to attract birders and other wildlife viewers.

It is important to note that an anthropocentrist would tolerate the extinction of a species if this brought about a large enough benefit to humanity or if another species could replace the role of the one that has been terminated. Because many songbirds have extremely similar diets, this latter point is a real possibility for many songbirds. The loss of one species could be ecologically compensated for by an increase in the population of other species.

Biocentrism maintains that humans are just one part of nature and that we have no right to exploit other organisms other than to meet our own basic needs. Thus, we should conserve birds because they have inherent value that is independent of whether they bring any benefits to humans. Ugly organisms, parasites, and economic "pests" are all considered just as valuable as charismatic songbirds. Biocentrists view the loss or decline of any bird species with alarm, particularly if "unnatural" human activities cause the population change. Biocentrist conservation, therefore, tends to emphasize "saving all the pieces" of an ecosystem and is generally not concerned with management of game animals. Biocentrists often try to maintain or restore ecosystems to their "natural" state. However, because humans have been part of the landscape of eastern North America for at least 10,000 years, it is hard to decide what is "natural." The biocentrist must then shift into the ambiguous territory of deciding what degree of human interference is desirable. Is a mix of 50% forest, 40% pasture, and 10% human habitations better or worse than 30% forest, 65% pasture, and 5% settlement? This debate is not just academic hairsplitting: Some biologists have taken the seemingly counterintuitive position of opposing designating parts of national forests as official wilderness areas. Logging, mining, and road building are banned in wilderness areas, and most environmental groups have pushed to establish more of these areas. The biologists who oppose these designations claim that some tree cutting is needed to maintain populations of birds that rely on young or shrubby forest habitat; thus, a wilderness designation would hurt these birds. Other biologists and conservation organizations have criticized this position, arguing that we already have enough young forest habitat but have so few roadless areas left that we should protect those that remain.

Conservation Biology, Policy, and Economics

Many eastern songbirds do face a conservation problem. As the examples in this chapter illustrate, declines of many songbird populations are due largely to competition with one other vertebrate: *Homo sapiens*. As the human population increases, such competition is likely to increase. All humans need space, food, and shelter. We compete with other organisms for these resources. Thus, as our own human population grows and as our per-capita use of resources increases, we will have negative effects on the other organisms that also use these limited resources. A stabilization of the human population would have enormous benefits for all kinds of biodiversity, as would a moderation in the excesses of our consumptive lifestyles.

Unfortunately for the birds, the human population looks set to continue increasing for at least another 100 years, and most humans show little interest in consuming less than they can afford. So what else might be done to help biodiversity? One answer to this question is to set aside protected areas such as parks, refuges, and sanctuaries. For example, large parts of the southern Appalachian Mountains are enclosed within either national parks or national forests. These public lands form a huge patch of relatively unbroken forest. Breeding birds in these areas are not subject to many of the negative effects of fragmentation described in this chapter, and for some species these protected areas may act as **source populations**: Bird populations in these areas are so successful that they provide colonists for **sink populations** that are not self-sustaining in forests in more fragmented parts of the country. Likewise, parks and protected areas on the migratory route and in the wintering grounds provide bird populations with some respite from the changes we have wrought on the rest of the landscape.

Parks cannot, however, provide the only answer. Humans need natural resources; thus, promoting bird-friendly use of our resources is a complementary approach to songbird conservation. The structure of our economy is not always on the side of the birds: All businesses have to make money, and birds do not generate much income. How, then, might resource extraction be made more bird friendly? One approach is for the government to regulate production practices. For example, in some states there are laws regulating how trees can be harvested from forests. These laws protect water quality and, some cases, protect the biodiversity of the forest community. Another example is the Endangered Species Act, which allows the government to protect species that have dwindled almost to oblivion (see Balch and Press, this volume). Government regulation is generally unpopular with those industries being regulated, and poorly designed laws may create as many problems as they solve. For example, landowners in the Southeast who do not wish to be regulated by the Endangered Species Act will sometimes log forests prematurely just to ensure that red-cockaded woodpeckers (an endangered species that lives in old pine forests) do not inhabit their land (Bonnie 1997). Nevertheless, in some cases regulation does provide an effective means of ensuring that commodity production does not trample too heavily on biodiversity.

Government regulation is not the only way to reform the economy. The forces of the marketplace can be harnessed in favor of the birds. The shade coffee example described earlier in this chapter provides one example of how consumers can help resource extraction industries make the transition to bird-friendly business practices. If all the bird lovers of the developed world bought shade-grown coffee and shunned sun-grown coffee, coffee production would be transformed into a more ecologically benign industry. The same principles apply to other areas. For example, timber companies differ in how they manage their forests. If there was a market for wood produced in a bird-friendly manner, consumers could reward those companies that practiced ecologically sound forestry (such as the Forest Stewardship Council 2000). Several factors stand in the way of allowing the force of the marketplace to bring about this sort of change. Unfortunately, most consumers are largely ignorant about the ways in which products are made and about the effects of production practices on other organisms. Thus, even the most ardent bird lovers have refrigerators stocked with orange juice from groves that have eliminated most the habitat of the Florida scrub jay, with coffee from plantations that have replaced tropical forests, with beef produced by degrading short-grass prairies, and with fish caught using methods that kill thousands of seabirds. Without knowledge, there can be no choice, and without choice, there can be no consumer-driven change. Thus, education is vitally important, but education is not enough. Even the most well-informed consumers can have no effect if products are not labeled so that consumers can make choices on the basis of their own values. With a few exceptions (such as shade coffee and organically grown food), most of our products betray no information about how they came to be. Wood from responsibly managed forests is stacked in lumber yards next to wood produced by pillage-and-run loggers, and the consumer has no way of distinguishing between the two. Informative labeling is rare because there are few financial incentives for industries to provide this source of information.

Despite these problems, some industries have realized that they can be responsible stewards of the land and increase sales by tapping the market for bird-friendly products. As more consumers and industry leaders recognize that they have the power to change how we make our living from the earth, we may be able to create an economy with room enough for humans, songbirds, and the rest of biodiversity.

R E F E R E N C E S

Bevanger, K. 1994. Bird interactions with utility structures: Collision and electrocution, causes and mitigating measures. *Ibis* 136:412–25.

Bonnie, R. 1997. Safe harbor for the red-cockaded woodpecker. *Journal of Forestry* 95:17–22.

Brittingham, M. C., and S. A. Temple. 1983. Have cowbirds caused forest songbirds to decline? *BioScience* 33:31–35.

Burke, D. M., and E. Nol. 1998. Influence of food abundance, nest-site habitat, and forest fragmentation on breeding ovenbirds. *Auk* 115:96–104.

Coker, D. R., and D. E. Capen. 1995. Landscape-level habitat use by brown-headed cowbirds in Vermont. *Journal of Wildlife Management* 59:631–37.

Crooks, K. R., and M. E. Soulé. 1999. Mesopredator release and avifaunal extinctions in a fragmented system. *Nature* 400:563–66.

Donovan, T. M., F. R. Thompson, J. Faaborg, and J. R. Probst. 1995. Reproductive success of migratory birds in habitat sources and sinks. *Conservation Biology* 9:1380–95.

Forest Stewardship Council. 2000. www.foreststewardship.org.

Gauthreaux, S. A. 1992. The use of weather radar to monitor long-term patterns of trans-Gulf migration in spring. In *Ecology and conservation of neotropical migrant landbirds*. Edited by J. M. Hagan and D. W. Johnston. Washington, D.C.: Smithsonian Institution Press, 96–100.

Greenberg, R., P. Bichier, A. C. Angon, and R. Reitsma. 1997. Bird populations in shade and sun coffee plantations in Central Guatemala. *Conservation Biology* 11:448–59.

Haskell, D. G. 2000. Effects of forest roads on macroinvertebrate soil fauna of the Southern Appalachians mountains. *Conservation Biology* 14:57–63.

Haskell, D. G., A. M. Knupp, and M. C. Schneider. 2001. Nest predator abundance and urbanization. In *Avian ecology and conservation in an urbanizing world*. Edited by J. M. Marzluff, R. Bowman, and R. Donnelly. Norwell, Mass.: Kluwer, 243–50.

Lynch, J. F. 1992. Distribution of overwintering Nearctic migrant in the Yucatan Peninsula, II: Use of native and human-modified vegetation. In *Ecology and conservation of neotropical migrant landbirds*. Edited by J. M. Hagan and D. W. Johnston. Washington, D.C.: Smithsonian Institution Press, 178–96.

Moguel, P., and V. M. Toledo. 1999. Biodiversity conservation in traditional coffee systems of Mexico. *Conservation Biology* 13:11–21.

Pearson, D. L., and S. S. Carroll. 1998. Global patterns of species richness: Spatial models for conservation planning using bioindicator and precipitation data. *Conservation Biology* 12:809–21.

Price, M. V., and J. T. Rotenberry. 2000. Single species as indicators of species richness and composition in California coastal sage scrub birds and small mammals. *Conservation Biology* 14:474–87.

Rice, R. A., and J. R. Ward. 1996. Coffee, conservation, and commerce in the Western Hemisphere. How individuals and institutions can promote ecologically sound farming and forest management in northern Latin America. Smithsonian Migratory Bird Center and Natural Resources Defense Council. www.si.edu/smbc/coffee/coffwhit.htm.

Robbins, C. W., B. A. Dowell, D. K. Dawson, J. A. Colón, R. Estrada, A. Sutton, R. Sutton, and D. Weyer. 1992. Comparison of neotropical migrant landbird populations wintering in tropical forest, isolated fragments, and agricultural habitats. In *Ecology and conservation of neotropical migrant landbirds*. Edited by J. M. Hagan and D. W. Johnston. Washington, D.C.: Smithsonian Institution Press, 207–10.

Robinson, S. K., F. R. Thompson, III, T. M. Donovan, D. R. Whitehead, and J. Faaborg. 1995. Regional forest fragmentation and the nesting success of migratory birds. *Science* 267:1987–90.

Rosenberg, K. V., J. D. Lowe, and A. A. Dhondt. 1999. Effects of forest fragmentation on breeding tanagers: A continental perspective. *Conservation Biology* 13:568–83.

Trine, C. L. 1998. Wood thrush population sinks and implications for the scale of regional conservation strategies. *Conservation Biology* 12:576–85.

Sauer, J. R., J. E. Hines, I. Thomas, J. Fallon, and G. Gough. 2000. *The North American Breeding Bird Survey, results and analysis 1966–1999*. Version 98.1. U.S. Geological Survey, Patuxent Wildlife Research Center, Laurel, Maryland. www.mbrpwrc.usgs.gov/bbs/bbs.html.

Sherry, T. W. 2000. Shade coffee: A good brew even in small doses. *Auk* 117:563–68.

Sutherland, W. J. 1998. Evidence for flexibility and constraint in migration systems. *Journal of Avian Biology* 29:441–46.

Uliczka, H., and P. Angelstam. 2000. Assessing conservation values of forest stands based on specialised lichens and birds. *Biological Conservation* 95:343–51.

Weber, T. P., and A. I. Houston. 1997. Flight costs, flight range and the stopover ecology of migrating birds. *Journal of Animal Ecology* 66:297–306.

Weber, T. P., A. I. Houston, and B. J. Ens. 1999. Consequences of habitat loss at migratory stopover sites: A theoretical investigation. *Journal of Avian Biology* 30:416–26.

Whitcomb R. F., C. S. Robbins, J. F. Lynch, B. L. Whitcomb, M. K. Klimkiewicz, and D. Bystrak. 1981. Effects of forest fragmentation on avifauna of eastern deciduous forest. In *Forest island dynamics in man-dominated landscapes.* Edited by R. L. Burgess and D. M. Sharpe. New York: Springer-Verlag, 125–205.

SUGGESTED READINGS

Hagan, J. M., III, and D. W. Johnston, eds. 1992. *Ecology and conservation of neotropical migrant landbirds.* Washington, D.C.: Smithsonian Institution Press.

Martin, T. E., and D. M. Finch, eds. 1995. *Ecology and management of neotropical migrant birds.* New York: Oxford University Press.

HAPTER

4

Valuing Nature

ETHICAL
PERSPECTIVES
ON THE LOSS
F BIODIVERSITY

Ben A. Minteer

On Arrowhead Mountain Lake, in northwestern Vermont, a breeding pair of mute swans established itself in 1993. The species, which evolved else-where (primarily in Europe and Asia), arrived in the United States around 1920, when several birds escaped from a private estate overseas. Not surprisingly, the swans are strikingly beautiful creatures, with their regal bearing, white plumage, and long S-shaped necks. But despite an aesthetic ideal that endows them with an almost fairy-tale tranquillity, the birds are, according to many wildlife managers and environmentalists, little more than obnoxious avian thugs. In particular, the swans are fiercely and often violently territorial. A single male will defend a range as large as 25 acres, driving out and often killing native bird species. They are also very heavy feeders, consuming 8 to 10 pounds of vegetation a day, which they procure, as one writer observed, by "using their feet like toilet plungers"—an activity that swirls out lake substrate and degrades water quality (Williams 1997, 27). Moreover, the birds' hostility is not reserved just for their fellow waterfowl. A growing litany of accounts describe the swans' habit of attacking biologists, boaters, and waterfront home owners. They seem to have a particular disdain for jet-skiers.

The mute swans in Vermont are part of a larger and potentially very serious national and international environmental problem—the reduction of local and global biodiversity as a result of the introduction of exotic or invasive plants and animals into native ecosystems. The swans on Arrowhead Mountain Lake are just one example of an exploding list of invasive species fanning out across the American landscape—from feral pigs in Hawaiian national parks and exotic trout in Yellowstone to the zebra mussels of the Great Lakes and the notorious cheat grass in the intermountain West. Such exotic introductions ultimately degrade the integrity of native species, and their presence can seriously disturb the functioning of natural ecological systems, eventually leading to the biologically disastrous "homogenization" of the global landscape (Baskin 1998). The handful of mute swans in Vermont therefore may be part of a greater and potentially alarming biological trend—the "alien invasion" of natural systems by nonnative plant and animals.

Given these considerations, when the population of swans on Arrowhead Mountain Lake expanded to eight birds in 1997, the Vermont Fish and Wildlife Department, charged with the management of the state's native species and their habitats, decided it had to take action. After holding a number of public hearings, the department announced its plan to kill the swans, a move that resulted in an immediate public firestorm. A group of lakeshore residents, under the auspices of their Arrowhead Mountain Lake Association, vehemently protested the department's proposed action, generating swarming media coverage (at least by Vermont standards) and drawing the attention of national animal rights organizations that promptly branded Vermont a "swan-killing state" (Williams 1997).

In response to such increasing public pressure and scrutiny, the department decided to attempt to capture the swans so that they might be shipped to a private conservation facility in Texas. This was easier said than done, however, and when the department was able to capture only two birds (at considerable effort and expense), it determined that this approach was not going to be a very practical or efficient means of handling the problem. The following summer, wildlife managers shot two of the six swans that returned to the lake, leading to greater public outcry and further straining the already hostile relationship between some of the public and the department.

The Vermont swan problem provides a good illustration of some of the issues relating to our understanding of biodiversity loss, especially the ambiguity of "biodiversity" as a measurable concept and the disagreements about which part or parts of such diversity, such as nonhuman entities or larger natural processes, are to be accorded primary value. With respect to the former concern, in one sense the arrival of the swans at Arrowhead Mountain Lake actually represented an *increase* in local biodiversity since their appearance effectively "added" one more population to the mix of flora and fauna in this particular Vermont ecosystem. Clearly, however, this local augmentation of species diversity was problematic from the standpoint of *native* waterfowl, which, when not competing with the invasive swans for food, were being driven from their habitat by the aggressive newcomers. Partly as a result of these sorts of situations, many biologists and ecologists have suggested that we need to recognize the critical distinction between "biodiversity," conceived as an aggregation of the genetic, individual, population, species, or ecosystemic diversity in a given area, and "biological integrity," defined as the ability of an identified ecological system to "generate and maintain adaptive biotic elements through natural evolutionary processes" (Angermeier and Karr 1996, 269). In this understanding, then, while the swans might have enhanced the local biodiversity at Arrowhead Mountain Lake (at least in the short run), they actually reduced the integrity of the ecosystem by degrading its natural systemic "wholeness," indicated by the "presence of all appropriate elements and occurrence of all [ecological and evolutionary] processes at appropriate rates" (Angermeier and Karr 1996, 266).

The considerable tension between some of the public and the state managers suggests that the swan dispute might also have stemmed from a deeper, more philosophical disagreement about the value placed on individual animals and ecological systems. Should we, for example, be solicitous of the welfare of individual swans and morally object to their "sacrifice" for the goal of protecting the biological integrity of the ecosystem? Or should we realize that the integrity of the other species and ecological processes of Arrowhead Mountain Lake has a certain priority over individual creatures (especially nonnative individuals), one that effectively "trumps" the lives of the swans in this case? Discussions about how best to manage our local, national, and global biological resources frequently evoke these kinds of value judgments regarding the comparative worth and hence the proper treatment of individual entities like swans and ecological systems like Arrowhead Mountain Lake. The consideration and justification of these sorts of claims deliver us squarely into the realm of **environmental ethics**, which we can think of as referring to a set of philosophical ideas about the appropriate relationship between humans and elements of the natural world.

A branch of applied, or practical philosophy, environmental ethics is still a very young academic field. Its origins owe primarily to a popular source—the increasing environmental concern and activism of the 1960s and 1970s and the recognition that the era's perceived "ecologic crisis" was as much a product of human value systems and philosophical commitments as it was a result of more immediate and overt material and technological problems (White 1967). The birth of professional environmental ethics during this period can also be seen as a direct outgrowth of the rise of other forms of applied philosophy in the early 1970s, a trend formally marked by the founding of the journal *Philosophy and Public Affairs* and the widespread turn to concrete social issues (such as abortion, warfare, famine, and so on) by moral and political philosophers.

Most contributors, however, trace the field's real *inspirational* roots to the pioneering work and thought of Aldo Leopold, a forester, wildlife biologist, conservationist, and amateur environmental philosopher whose book *A Sand County Almanac* (1949) triggered what is generally considered a Copernican change in our conceptualization of the human place in the natural world. In *Sand County*, Leopold provided a poetically rich and morally powerful argument for why human society must seek a more thoughtful, principled relationship with the environment. This new relationship was to be governed by what he referred to as a "land ethic," an ecological worldview supporting a set of moral claims that directed us to take a more expansive and intelligent account of the myriad interdependencies between human and natural communities. While contemporary environmental ethicists (such as Callicott 1989; Norton 1996) have often disagreed over the precise philosophical meaning of Leopold's observations and directives in this little book, his influence on the field's professional development has been profound, and his integrated moral and scientific vision continues to stoke the fires of our collective environmental imagination.

Leopold's legacy was evoked in what most consider to be the first paper written by a professional philosopher about environmental ethics, "Is There a Need for a New, an Environmental, Ethic?" by the Australian Richard Routley (later Sylvan) in 1973. Since Routley's paper has cast a long shadow over much of the work in environmental ethics in the ensuing decades, it is worthwhile to briefly mention its main thesis before we move to a more systematic discussion of environmental ethical theory. The paper's significance is perhaps best summed up by Routley's memorable "last man" example, which he employed as a kind of thought experiment to expose the environmental failings of conventional, humanistic ethical systems. As he wrote, according to the traditional moral commitments of Western civilization, the last man surviving the collapse of the world system would, in fact, be committing no wrong if he set about destroying every species of animal and plant on earth. Since only humans have value in Western ethics and since nature is therefore viewed as essentially valueless, we have no governing set of moral principles that will allow us to condemn such wanton destructiveness (Routley 1973). Indeed, Routley leveled a harsh indictment against the Western philosophical tradition, particularly for this "human chauvinism" he found lying in its exclusive concern for human interests. To Routley's mind, this was a regrettable, if not a pernicious, bias that explained the arrogance and abuse humans have historically demonstrated toward nonhuman nature. Routley thus offered an unambiguous reply to the question contained in his paper's title: A new ethics *was* needed if we were serious about taking the good of the environment into account in our deliberations over the rightness and wrongness of human treatment of the earth's biological resources. As mentioned earlier, his argument on this count was very influential in setting the conceptual and practical agenda for much subsequent work in environmental ethics. Specifically, in this early paper, Routley was calling for the rejection of what environmental ethicists would later term the worldview of **anthropocentrism** (literally, "human centeredness") and the purely **instrumental value** of nature in favor of the worldview of **nonanthropocentrism** ("life centeredness" or "ecologically centeredness") and a recognition of nature's **intrinsic value**.

While Routley's desire to jettison the humanism running through Western philosophy became the rallying cry of most environmental ethicists, it is important to note that there was by no means a complete acceptance of the necessity of this task in the field's formative period. One year after Routley's paper first appeared, for example, his fellow Australian John Passmore published the first book-length treatment of environmental ethics, *Man's Responsibility for Nature* (1974). Unlike Routley, Passmore claimed that conventional Western ethical traditions, even though they focus chiefly on aspects of human rather than nonhuman interests, nevertheless are sufficient grounds for calling our treatment of nature into question. In other words, according to Passmore, we do not have to reject anthropocentrism on the path to environmental reform; we simply need to take fuller account of how destructive environmental practices negatively impact the aesthetic and moral commitments we hold dear within the human community. Passmore's early treatment of environmental ethics thus stands as a counterpoint to Routley's and others' contention that only a nonanthropocentric worldview is capable of supporting an improved human–nature relationship.

With these early and general historical foundations in mind, let us now move to a somewhat more detailed discussion of the major conceptual distinctions and theoretical positions in environmental ethics since an acquaintance with them is critical to understanding how the field's contributors view the problem of biodiversity loss.

Environmental Ethical Theory

It is helpful to think of the most historically influential approaches in environmental ethics as falling in the two general worldviews mentioned previously, each of which may be further classified into two or more additional sets of positions: anthropocentric (human-centered) approaches, which include 1) strong anthropocentric positions and 2) **weak anthropocentric/pragmatic** positions, and nonanthropocentric (nonhuman-centered) approaches, which include 1) **zoocentric** (animal-centered) positions, 2) **biocentric** (life-centered) positions, and 3) **ecocentric** (ecologically centered) positions.

ANTHROPOCENTRIC APPROACHES

Strong Anthropocentrism

A strong anthropocentrist views nature primarily in terms of its (usually immediate- and/or short-term) usefulness in satisfying human consumer preferences. Under this position, nature has no intrinsic value or no value independent of direct human uses and desires. In other words, for a strong anthropocentrist, nature can have only a narrowly *instrumental* value, especially in a consumptive sense: It is merely a material means to human-defined ends. So, for example, a strong anthropocentrist would regard the biological richness of an old-growth forest as little more than an inventory of potential board feet of timber, the harvesting and selling of which enhances human welfare (measured in purely economic terms). Many environmental ethicists (such as Katz 1979; Sagoff 1988) conflate this attitude with the general moral principle of **utilitarianism**, which directs individuals to endorse those actions that maximize the greatest aggregate good, defined as exclusively human pleasure, happiness, or some other welfare-regarding concept. It is safe to say that nearly all environmental ethicists are united in the belief that strong anthropocentrism not only is not an inadequate ground for conceiving of our relationship to the environment but also the very attitude that has led to the acceleration of biodiversity loss and the decline in environmental health and integrity more broadly.

Weak Anthropocentrism/Pragmatism

While recognizing the unacceptable environmental implications of strong anthropocentrism, some theorists, in a spirit sympathetic to Passmore's early argument, have suggested that an anthropocentric worldview need not be crassly consumptive or exploitative of nonhuman nature. The environmental philosopher Bryan Norton, for example, introduced the notion of what he called a "weaker" version of anthropocentrism to the field in the mid-1980s, a more thoughtful and environmentally sensitive humanism that seemed to avoid the antienvironmental consequences of harshly utilitarian-style ethical positions regarding nonhuman nature (Norton 1984). According to Norton's argument, unlike advocates of strong anthropocentrism, the "weak anthropocentrist" does not simply seek to press nature into the service of a set of "demand values" in the form of immediate material goods and services (such as board feet from a forest). Instead, she may recognize that nature possesses what Norton dubbed "transformative value." This concept refers to the notion that contact and experience with nature allows individuals to critically evaluate and eventually *transform* their exploitative, consumer-centered preferences into more environmentally benign, "considered preferences," or ideals that are compatible with an ecologically enlightened worldview. Such a move allows Norton to retain an anthropocentric outlook (since his position does not directly and unequivocally attribute independent value to elements and processes of the natural world) while rejecting the reduction of all environmental values to consumer goods (Norton 1987). In recent years, and as we will discuss in more detail in the next section, Norton has expanded this weak anthropocentric position to embrace a more explicitly pragmatic approach. Specifically, and following the lead of earlier classical American pragmatists like Charles Sanders Peirce, William James, and John Dewey, Norton has argued for a more "practical" and policy-driven spirit in environmental ethics (Norton 1995, 1996, 1999). The tendency for many of the field's contributors to dwell on abstract and often ideological value debates and conflicts has, according to Norton and pragmatic observers like Light (1996), Minteer (1998), and Weston (1992), actually diverted ethicists' attention away from real-world environmental problems. As a result, many "environmental pragmatists" suggest that potential areas of agreement and common ground among environmentalists of varying ethical stripes go missing. The pragmatic approach is perhaps most succinctly demonstrated by Norton's "convergence hypothesis," an attempt to highlight what he takes to be an emerging consensus among environmental philosophers, professionals, and environmentally concerned citizens. We will consider Norton's hypothesis and its role in biodiversity valuation in the next section.

In addition to Norton, Eugene Hargrove (1992) has also offered an account of weak anthropocentrism that, like Norton's, claims that when we go about valuing nature, we necessarily must do so from an anthropocentric standpoint. Unlike Norton's version of weak anthropocentrism, however, Hargrove's incarnation features a robust theory of the intrinsic value of natural objects, a position he nevertheless justifies *anthropocentrically*. Specifically, and against those contributors like Routley who find no moral resources for environmentalism in the Western philosophic and cultural canon, Hargrove grounds his approach in the naturalistic traditions of 19th-century landscape painting and field naturalism. According to Hargrove, we may ascribe intrinsic value to those elements of nature we judge to be beautiful or scientifically interesting, though such ascription is made from a distinctly human point of view (Hargrove 1989). Despite this humanistic orientation, Hargrove has made it clear that his approach has little to do with more pragmatic variants of weak anthropocentrism (Hargrove 1992).

While weak anthropocentric positions represent significant departures from environmentally exploitative forms of human centeredness—what David Ehrenfield (1978) memorably referred to as "arrogant humanism"—many environmental ethicists, following in the earlier footsteps of Routley, believe that they are inadequate responses to the philosophical condition lying at the root of modern environmental crises such as biodiversity loss and ecological degradation. Instead, most of these theorists argue that a wholesale rejection of anthropocentrism and an adoption of some form of nonanthropocentrism are required if we are truly serious about reforming our environmental attitudes and practices.

NONANTHROPOCENTRIC POSITIONS

Zoocentrism

This category refers to animal welfare/rights positions, like the influential projects advanced by philosophers Tom Regan (1983) and Peter Singer (1975). While many environmental ethicists refuse to include zoocentric positions in the *formal* definition of environmental ethics because they are thought to be insufficiently sensitive to the values of the broader biotic community, it is clear that such views fall within the parameters of the nonanthropocentric worldview and therefore are best included in more generous and ecumenical discussions of environmental ethics. Singer's **animal welfare** or **animal liberation** approach is concerned primarily with the human infliction of suffering on individual animals conscious enough to experience states of pleasure and pain or those creatures that are sentient. Singer argues that we must recognize that these sentient animals have *interests* and that these interests should always be taken into account when we make decisions affecting animal welfare. More to the point, he believes that a morally repugnant "speciesism" pervades the human community, a discriminatory attitude analogous to racism or sexism that allows us to justify what is actually a philosophically indefensible neglect of animals' interests. While Singer does not make any attempt to claim that animals must in all cases be treated as *literal* equals to humans, he does argue that their interests deserve *equal consideration.* To serve this task, Singer marshals and extends the philosophical principle of utilitarianism in this quest for the improvement of animal welfare. Rather than looking to bring about the greatest beneficial consequences for individual humans, however, Singer expands the utilitarian principle to include the goal of maximizing the pleasure (or in some cases the preferences) of *all* sentient creatures, a big moral "tent" that includes a wide array of nonhuman animals. Regan's version of zoocentrism is properly termed an **animal rights** position, even though the designation is often (mistakenly) used to refer to any and all ethical arguments calling for the fair treatment of animals. Where Singer places the threshold for the moral consideration of an entity at sentience, Regan prefers to place the bar of moral consideration somewhat higher. For Regan, those animals that are sufficiently conscious and are able to have what we would think of as beliefs and desires are to be accorded direct moral consideration. According to Regan, these beings are "experiencing subjects of a life" (a class including human individuals but also all "mentally normal mammals of a year or older") and are therefore "ends-in-themselves" that should not be treated as mere resources for human satisfaction. Not surprisingly, Regan is categorically against sport hunting, commercial agriculture involving animals, and the use of animals in invasive forms of biomedical experimentation (Regan 1983).

Biocentrism

This category is often employed rather indiscriminately to refer to all versions of nonanthropocentrism, but it is more properly understood as a description of *individualistic,* "life-centered" nonanthropocentric approaches like that of biocentrism's most influential expositor, Paul Taylor (1986). Taylor claims that those individual organisms that are "teleological centers of life," that is, those entities that are goal directed, have a "good of their own" that can be frustrated or encouraged by human moral agents. In Taylor's view, for example, a tree has the "goal" of growing to full maturity; this "good" is therefore violated by those who would seek to cut it down for human benefit. As a consequence of this goal directedness and of having a good of their own, individual plants, trees, animals, and humans possess what Taylor calls "inherent worth." Since, according to Taylor, all individuals that are goal directed have equal inherent worth, his overarching belief system—what he refers to as the "biocentric outlook on nature"—endorses a bold species egalitarianism that deprivileges humans in the natural order. It follows from Taylor's argument that biological and ecological collectives like species, communities, and ecosystems thus have value only to the extent that they are aggregates of individual creatures possessing inherent worth. While Taylor's 1986 book *Respect for Nature* still remains the most synoptic and eloquent treatment of **biocentric individualism** in the field, more recent biocentric devotees like James Sterba (1998) and Gary Varner (1998) have advanced this nonanthropocentric position (though in quite different ways) in environmental ethics.

Ecocentrism

This final set of basic positions in environmental ethics is probably the most widely endorsed and professionally emblematic orientation in the field, especially since two of ecocentrism's main proponents, Holmes Rolston, III and J. Baird Callicott, have been leading voices in environmental ethics since the establishment of the flagship journal of the same name in 1979. Ecocentric positions like Rolston's and Callicott's place ultimate (that is, intrinsic) value in ecological communities (rather than individual organisms), although they often differ over whether such value is projected onto natural systems by human valuers (a *subjectivist* position pre-

ferred by Callicott) or whether it actually resides in the systems themselves, independent of human valuation (an *objectivist* position advanced
by Rolston). Rolston, too, seems to place a higher degree of value than Callicott on the various "subelements" of the biological hierarchy, locating intrinsic value in individual plants, animals, and species while reserving the
"highest" regard for the projective, "systemic value" of ecological wholes
(Rolston 1988, 1994). Callicott has drawn direct philosophical inspiration
for his ecocentric position from Leopold's land ethic mentioned earlier.
Specifically, Callicott reads Leopold's approach in strongly nonanthropocentric terms, interpreting the great conservationist's ideas as pointing
toward a moral duty to protect ecological systems for their own rather
than human benefit (Callicott 1989, 1999). Callicott's early and somewhat
strident statement of his "Leopoldian" nonanthropocentric holism (Callicott 1980) led to charges of "ecological fascism" by ethical individualists
like Tom Regan, who worried that the moral priority placed on ecological
collectives would lead, in some situations, to the sacrifice of individual animals if ecological goals demanded it (Regan 1983). In response to these
sorts of objections, Callicott has since softened the misanthropic language
of his earlier argument, claiming that his understanding of ethical holism
is not at all closed to ethical regard for either human or nonhuman individuals (Callicott 1999).

Valuing Biodiversity in Environmental Ethics

Given the philosophical heterogeneity of the positions just sketched, it is
perhaps not surprising that environmental ethicists often disagree about
the best conceptual and practical approaches to take in biodiversity valuation. As we saw earlier, many times these disagreements surround the determination of the appropriate "level" or "unit" of moral concern, that is,
whether we should pay comparatively more attention to the value of individual organisms, higher animals, species, or ecosystems. When these
fairly abstract value questions become translated into the real-world

realm of environmental policy, they concern what we might think of as "conservation targets" (Norton 1994), that is, the specific biotic elements and/or processes we are trying to save from anthropogenic, or human-caused, destruction.

For example, many environmental ethicists have raised serious doubts about the usefulness of zoocentric positions in underwriting the protection of biodiversity, especially for addressing the biotic and ecological concerns at the broader level of the natural community or ecosystem. An interesting illustration of this division, and one that echoes the value conflict in the mute swan dilemma mentioned at the beginning of this chapter, may be found in a recent critical anthology of papers devoted to analyzing the previously mentioned work of animal liberationist Peter Singer (Jamieson 1999). In his contribution to the Singer volume, Holmes Rolston, a leading proponent of ecocentrism, points out what he takes to be the *environmental* inadequacy of Singer's central moral argument regarding the human treatment of animals: the latter's notion that we must apply a "principle of equality" to all (and only those) sentient creatures. Rolston suggests that such a position clearly lacks the sort of *holistic* or *systemic* understanding of value that would morally enfranchise the full sweep of natural elements and processes that extend above and beyond the community of sentient creatures. Specifically, in his view,

> The trouble [with Singer's argument] is that this is not a systemic view of what is going on on the valuable Earth we now experience, before we experienced it. We need an account of the generation of value and valuers, not just some value that now is located in the psychology of the experiencers. Finding that value will generate an Earth Ethics, with a global sense of obligation to this whole inhabited planet. The evolution of rocks into dirt and dirt into fauna and flora is one of the great surprises of natural history, one of the rarest events in the astronomical universe. . . . At this scale of vision, if we ask what is principally to be valued, the value of life arising as a creative process on Earth seems a better description and a more comprehensive category than the pains and pleasures of a fractional percentage of its inhabitants. (Rolston 1999, 266–67)

Rolston thinks that Singer's preoccupation with the welfare of *individual* animals stops far short of providing an effective moral argument for the large-scale ecological *processes* that the former believes to be the source of all value in nature. In response, Singer denies that his animal liberation position is unable to take account of the value of nonsentient parts of the environment, disagreeing with Rolston's interpretation that such a focus precludes him from expressing any concern about the condition of natural elements like plants and trees, biological collectives like species, and macrolevel processes like atmospheric integrity. Specifically, Singer argues that he is able to morally consider these "nonfeeling" parts of the environment by assessing the degree to which their loss leads to the harm of those pleasure and pain-experiencing animals who depend on them (Singer 1999). For example, since the destruction of a forest community for economic development clearly harms those sentient animals that look to such systems for food and shelter, Singer can therefore still claim that the development of the forest is ethically wrong, even if the bulldozers do not actually roll over its pain-feeling vertebrates in the process.

Moreover, he believes that his position regarding the moral claims placed on us by sentient individuals is not his only ground for judging the appropriateness of specific behaviors and policies that affect the environment. Specifically, at the conclusion of his response to Rolston, Singer observes that he may also choose to argue that actions such as the wanton destruction of plants, trees, species, and entire ecosystems are wrong because they deny the "precious heritage that we should preserve in order to pass on to our children and grandchildren" (Singer 1999, 332). Singer's remark here suggests an ethical approach to the environment that, rather than assuming a *direct* concern with its constituent nonhuman members or ecological processes, adopts instead an *indirect* commitment to nature through a concern for the environment's contribution to the overall quality of life of future generations of humans. Singer and Rolston clearly disagree over what part of nonhuman nature is to be accorded primary value and that this disagreement seems to lead them to recognize different duties and/or obligations to elements of biodiversity.

This disagreement between Singer and Rolston is by no means an isolated or trivial dispute in discussions about biodiversity valuation. But since most environmental ethicists subscribe to some sort of holistic approach to environmental values, it is probably of less import than the long-standing and occasionally vocal dispute that exists *within* the holist/systemic camp over whether a nonanthropocentric or an anthropocentric regard for ecological systems is required to support sound environmental protection. One of the more intriguing discussions about the moral justification of policies to protect biological resources has concerned Norton's convergence hypothesis, mentioned in the previous section. This project is most systematically developed in his book *Toward Unity among Environmentalists* (1991), but it has also been featured in several more recent articles (Norton 1995, 1996, 1997). Norton's claim, which he advances as "a general empirical hypothesis about policy" (Norton 1997, 99), is fairly straightforward. In a nutshell, the convergence argument predicts that 1) *if* certain individuals are consistent "broad anthropocentrists" (in this context, **moral pluralists** who embrace the full range of human values in nature, such as aesthetic, spiritual, recreational, and educational, *over time*) and 2) *if* certain other individuals are nonanthropocentrists who, like Callicott and Rolston, endorse a consistent notion of the intrinsic value of nature, then 3) *both* positions will "converge" on a common policy direction in practice. Norton predicts this convergence because he believes that both the broad anthropocentric camp and the nonanthropocentric camp embrace values that are dependent on the long-term ecological sustainability of natural systems. This common policy goal, Norton suggests, centers on the protection of creative ecosystem dynamics because the maintenance of multigenerational ecological processes is the only way to preserve biological diversity over the long run, whether for the benefit of future generations of humans or for the value that such diversity possesses in or for itself (Norton and Ulanowicz 1992). Since Norton also concludes that there are a number of thorny philosophical problems afflicting nonanthropocentric theory (Norton 1995), he claims that it is more practical and effective to argue for biodiversity protection from the broad anthropocentric, or *pragmatic*, point of view, a position that is not wedded to any argument advancing the notion that nonhuman nature carries human-independent, or intrinsic, value.

Norton's argument for convergence—and its implications for biodiversity valuation and policymaking—has generated a fair amount of controversy in environmental ethics. Ecocentric theorists have generally not accepted the validity of Norton's prediction regarding the convergence of anthropocentric and nonanthropocentric positions. Callicott, for example, has expressed his disagreement with relying on the convergence hypothesis as a guide to biodiversity protection in no uncertain terms:

> Norton's "convergence hypothesis" . . . is dead wrong. If all environmental values are anthropocentric and instrumental, then they have to compete head to head with economic values derived from converting rain forests to lumber and pulp, savannas to cattle pasture, and so on. Environmentalists, in other words, must show that preserving biological diversity is of greater instrumental value to present and future human generations than is lucrative timber extraction, agricultural conversion, hydroelectric impoundments, mining, and so on. For this simple reason, a persuasive philosophical case for the intrinsic value of nonhuman natural entities and nature as a whole would make a huge practical difference. (Callicott 1999, 31)

Callicott clearly believes that a nonanthropocentric orientation toward biodiversity protection is more philosophically defensible and effective. Indeed, in his view granting intrinsic value to nature makes a "huge practical difference" when it comes to justifying policies that protect biological resources. Callicott therefore denies that ecocentric and broad anthropocentric positions will "converge" on similar goals and environmental policies since the latter (such as multivocal arguments for the recreational, aesthetic, or educational value of nature) will always be held hostage to more powerful commercial values in real experience. Callicott's skepticism about Norton's project is shared by other nonanthropocentric holists, such as Laura Westra (1997), who, similar to Callicott, assumes that a commitment to a strong theory of intrinsic value located in ecological systems (what she refers to as the "principle of integrity") is necessary to the making of any effective ethical argument for the protection of nature.

Is Norton right in predicting the likely converge of environmental ethical positions on multigenerational ecosystemic-based policies? While nonanthropocentric critics like Callicott and Westra have spent a great deal of time homing in on what they take to be the philosophical flaws in Norton's hypothesis, they have generally paid less attention to the *empirical* side of his argument, that is, whether the hypothesis actually holds in specific real-world cases. On this score, some early evidence is emerging that suggests Norton's hypothesis is experientially valid, at least in particular cases. To mention but one example, Minteer and Manning (2000) have conducted a study of the relationship between the Vermont public's environmental ethical commitments and their attitudes toward specific policy alternatives for the management of the state's national forest, an investigation that lends strong local support to Norton's argument. The Vermont study findings indicate that while residents supported a diverse mix of ethical stances regarding nonhuman nature (including "broad anthropocentric," "biocentric," and "ecocentric" positions), they generally tended to endorse a common policy direction for the Green Mountain National Forest. This policy orientation emphasized the protection of ecosystem-level processes over the long term as well as the safeguarding of fish and wildlife habitat and plant and animal diversity, features that mirror Norton's discussion of multiscalar environmental management (Norton and Ulanowicz 1992).

Norton's convergence argument is a more pragmatic approach to environmental ethics in that it does not focus on fixed philosophical principles or foundational moral claims about the natural world but rather looks for areas of public value compatibility and political common ground in the environmental policy arena. While evidence like that provided by the Vermont study suggests that support for a common policy direction may emerge out of a diversity of environmental value commitments, clearly additional empirical investigation is required if Norton's thesis is to be widely endorsed as a reliable guide to thinking about the relationship between environmental ethics and policy choices. Nevertheless, his approach is one of the more visible examples of an emerging pragmatic emphasis within the field of environmental ethics on the importance of building diverse and morally inclusive coalitions for biological conservation and environmental protection.

With this pragmatic spirit in mind, let us return to the mute Vermont swan problem described in the beginning of this chapter. Will this dilemma, which has important implications for local biodiversity, be settled by appealing to the intrinsic value of the nonnative birds or the ecosystem? Actually, if we consider the mute swan case in greater detail, we see that some common ground between the state wildlife officials and the lakeshore residents regarding what to do about these biological "invaders" did, in fact, exist. Their comments in the local newspapers revealed that many of the members of the Arrowhead Mountain Lake Association recognized the potentially undesirable effects the swans could have on the health and integrity of the lake system. Furthermore, a number of them believed that some sort of control action might be necessary. What many contested was therefore not the ecological reality of the problem but rather the *method* of control (shooting) devised by the Fish and Wildlife Department to handle the bird situation. Alternatively, many residents spoke of wanting to manage the bird problem themselves by shaking or "addling" their eggs in their nests, considered by many observers to be a reasonable form of swan birth control (Allen 1998). This suggests that, following Norton, the goal of maintaining a healthy Arrowhead Mountain Lake united both camps and that we risk losing sight of this public consensus if we overemphasize the importance of conflicting environmental ethical attachments in the abstract. While such pragmatic stances like Norton's have gained momentum in the field (see Light and Katz 1996), it is safe to say that nonanthropocentric positions remain the dominant approach in environmental ethics. Callicott, for instance, has referred to Norton's pragmatism as "antiphilosophy" since it tries to look past many of the foundational value questions that have historically occupied the field's intellectual attention (Callicott 1999). The liveliness of this particular philosophical debate is perhaps an indication of the high stakes lying at its core, namely, the determination of the most practically effective and intellectually defensible way to justify the protection of biological resources in public discourse and policy deliberations. It is an argument that is likely to continue in environmental ethics for many years to come.

Conclusion

The field of environmental ethics is still in its youth; it is "green" in more than just the ideological sense. Despite this, it is clear that a number of philosophically compelling projects have been advanced over the past three decades that promise to offer strong moral justifications for protecting local, national, and global biodiversity. Whether they are committed weak anthropocentrists, biocentrists, ecocentrists, or something else altogether, environmental ethicists are nonetheless all united in pursuing a more biologically diverse and healthy landscape—they simply differ on some of the (rather technical) philosophical details attending to this shared practical goal. This is not to say that such differences are insignificant; indeed, they are often quite striking. Doubtless many of these positions would lead to visibly divergent human–nature relationships if systematically (and consistently) implemented in practice. But it is still safe to say that environmental ethicists are nowhere arguing that much *less* biodiversity is desirable in the world, regardless of whether they defend their claims from a broad anthropocentric or nonanthropocentric point of view. This is a more general and perhaps even more powerful example of "convergence" that continues to unfold as the field moves toward professional maturity in the 21st century.

REFERENCES

Allen, A. 1998. Group protests swan kill. *Burlington Free Press*, April 10, 1B, 6.

Angermeier, P. L., and J. R. Karr. 1996. Biological integrity versus biological diversity as policy directives: Protecting biotic resources. In *Ecosystem*

Management. Edited by F. Samson and F. Knopf. New York: Springer, 264–75.

Baskin, Y. 1998. *The work of nature: How the diversity of life supports us.* Washington, D.C.: Island Press.

Callicott, J. B. 1980. Animal liberation: A triangular affair. *Environmental Ethics* 2:311–38.

———. 1989. *In defense of the land ethic.* Albany: State University of New York Press.

———. 1999. *Beyond the land ethic: More essays in environmental philosophy.* Albany: State University of New York Press.

Ehrenfeld, D. 1978. *The arrogance of humanism.* New York: Oxford University Press.

Hargrove, E. 1989. *Foundations of environmental ethics.* Englewood Cliffs, N.J.: Prentice Hall.

———. 1992. Weak anthropocentric intrinsic value. *The Monist* 75:183–207.

Jamieson, D., ed. 1999. *Singer and his critics.* Oxford: Blackwell.

Katz, E. 1979. Utilitarianism and preservation. *Environmental Ethics* 1:357–64.

Leopold, A. 1949. *A Sand County almanac and sketches here and there.* New York: Oxford University Press.

Light, A. 1996. Compatibilism in political ecology. In *Environmental pragmatism.* Edited by A. Light and E. Katz. London: Routledge, 161–84.

Light, A., and E. Katz, eds. 1996. *Environmental pragmatism.* London: Routledge.

Minteer, B. A. 1998. No experience necessary? Foundationalism and the retreat from culture in environmental ethics. *Environmental Values* 7:338–48.

Minteer, B. A., and R. E. Manning. 2000. Convergence in environmental values: An empirical and conceptual defense. *Ethics, Place and Environment* 3:47–60.

Norton, B. 1984. Environmental ethics and weak anthropocentrism. *Environmental Ethics* 6:131–48.

———. 1987. *Why preserve natural variety?* Princeton, N.J.: Princeton University Press.

———. 1991. *Toward unity among environmentalists.* Oxford: Oxford University Press.

———. 1994. On what we should save: The role of culture in determining conservation targets. In *Systematics and conservation evaluation.* Edited by P. Forey, C. Humphries, and R. Vane-wright. Oxford: Clarendon, 23–40.

———. 1995. Why I am not a nonanthropocentrist: Callicott and the failure of monistic inherentism. *Environmental Ethics* 17:341–58.

———. 1996. The constancy of Leopold's land ethic. In *Environmental pragmatism*. Edited by A. Light and E. Katz. London: Routledge, 84–102.

———. 1997. Convergence and contextualism: Some clarifications and a reply to Steverson. *Environmental Ethics* 19:87–100.

———. 1999. Pragmatism, adaptive management, and sustainability. *Environmental Values* 8:451–66.

Norton, B., and R. Ulanowicz. 1992. Scale and biodiversity policy: A hierarchical approach. *Ambio* 21:244–49.

Passmore, J. 1974. *Man's responsibility for nature.* New York: Scribner.

Regan, T. 1983. *The case for animal rights.* Berkeley: University of California Press.

Rolston, H., III. 1988. *Environmental ethics.* Philadelphia: Temple University Press.

———. 1994. *Conserving natural value.* New York: Columbia University Press.

———. 1999. Respect for life: Counting what Singer finds of no account. In *Singer and his critics*. Edited by D. Jamieson. Oxford: Blackwell, 247–68.

Routley, R. 1973. Is there a need for a new, and environmental ethic? *Proceedings of the 15th World Congress of Philosophy* 1:205–10.

Sagoff, M. 1988. *The economy of the earth.* Cambridge: Cambridge University Press.

Singer, P. 1975. *Animal liberation: A new ethics for our treatment of animals.* New York: Avon.

———. 1999. A response. In *Singer and his critics*. Edited by D. Jamieson. Oxford: Blackwell, 269–335.

Sterba, J. 1998. A biocentrist strikes back. *Environmental Ethics* 20:361–76.

Taylor, P. 1986. *Respect for nature.* Princeton, N.J.: Princeton University Press.

Varner, G. 1998. *In nature's interests?* Oxford: Oxford University Press.

Weston, A. 1992. *Toward better problems.* Philadelphia: Temple University Press.

Westra, L. 1997. Why Norton's approach is insufficient for environmental ethics. *Environmental Ethics* 19:279–97.

White, L. 1967. The historical roots of our ecologic crisis. *Science* 155:1203–7.

Williams, T. 1997. The ugly swan. *Audubon*, November–December, 26–32.

SUGGESTED READINGS

Brennan, A. 1988. *Thinking about nature: An investigation into nature, value, and ecology.* Athens: University of Georgia Press.

Hayward, T. 1998. *Political theory and ecological values.* New York: St. Martin's.

O'Neill, J. 1993. *Ecology, policy and politics: Human well-being and the natural world.* New York: Routledge.

Stone, C. 1987. *Earth and other ethics: The case for moral pluralism.* New York: Harper & Row.

Taylor, B. P. 1992. *Our limits transgressed: Environmental political thought in America.* Lawrence: University Press of Kansas.

Wenz, P. 1988. *Environmental justice.* Albany: State University of New York Press.

5

Pricing Protection

NDERSTANDING
THE
NVIRONMENTAL
CONOMICS OF
BIODIVERSITY
PROTECTION

David A. Anderson

Although many people associate it with money, **economics** is fundamentally about the allocation of scarce resources among competing ends. The components of biological diversity represent scarce resources, making biodiversity a natural candidate for economic analysis. Stepping back from the problem, it is clear that several of the causes of biodiversity loss—development, policy failure, and market failure—are themselves appropriately addressed using the tools of economics. The economic literature is replete with estimates of the value of biodiversity, studies of the determinants of diversity loss, proposals for the prioritization of biodiversity, and analysis of public policy designed to manage diversity. This chapter explains some of the common models and approaches economists use to address issues of biodiversity and highlights some of the significant findings.

Economic Approaches and Paradigms

COST-BENEFIT ANALYSIS

Cost-benefit analysis is perhaps the most obvious economic tool to apply when the question is, How much biodiversity loss is too much? Before this concept can be explored, two related items must be explained. First, it should be clear that the costs and benefits we refer to in economic analysis are not necessarily in dollars per se. Financial analysis of natural areas that looks at the flow of money associated with parks or other wilderness areas is only a subset of economic valuation, which measures both market and nonmarket values of resources. The benefits associated with preserving animal species, for example, might include a warm feeling in our hearts and the joy of being able to introduce our children to these animals in addition to the profits from ecotourism, medical cures, and so on. For simplicity, it is common to value all the costs and benefits in terms of dollars. Emotional and other nonmonetary concerns are not neglected; they are simply measured in terms of a standard unit—dollars—for comparison.

The second item to be understood is that economic approaches typically have **efficiency** as a goal. In regard to environmental issues, this is a departure from a more simplistic view that either production should be maximized or pollution/habitat loss should be minimized. The best outcome for society is neither the highest possible level of production nor zero pollution. The singular goal of maximizing production would likely decrease the welfare of society as we encountered smoke-blackened skies, failing health, and the absence of wildlife—all sacrificed in the name of productivity. At the same time, the first puff of smoke from a chimney may permit a newborn baby to have enough warmth to survive while imposing no significant effects on the environment. Some amount of pollution is desirable to enable the existence of hospitals and schools, food production, and a basic standard of living. A goal of efficiency can lead to what is best for society as a whole in a way that rigid pro-business or pro-environment positions do not.

Although biodiversity could be quantified in a number of ways, for the purpose of this chapter it will be measured in terms of the number of species preserved. The same conclusions would apply to most alternative measures as well. In general, it is likely that the additional cost of preserving one more species will increase as more and more species are preserved. We start with easy conservation efforts and then move on to more difficult ones. The first habitat destruction forgone will be the least important (we give up a go-cart track before a hospital), the first hours volunteered for environmental cleanup will be the least valuable (time otherwise spent watching television, not researching cures for cancer), and the requirements of the easiest-to-preserve species (types of cockroaches) are far lower than those for more vulnerable species (the northern spotted owl). As more and more species are preserved, more and more valuable alternatives will be forgone. The housing, transportation, diet, and material possessions typical in developed countries all exact tolls on other living things. To preserve *all* biodiversity would require tremendous sacrifices in terms of the conditions for human existence. In some cases, biodiversity loss results from a conscious decision to substitute a desired set of man-made assets (like a subdivision) for a set of natural assets.

While the costs of preserving additional species increase as more and more are preserved, the corresponding benefits are likely to decrease. The species with the highest priority for preservation, presumably *Homo sapiens*, is clearly valued quite highly. Additional species provide great benefits, but the more we have, the less of a contribution an additional species makes to available diversity. The first species of butterfly contributes to diversity in a way that the ten-thousandth does not. The theorized decreasing additional benefits and increasing additional costs of preserving species are graphed in figure 5.1. The corresponding *total* benefits from preserving various numbers of species, as opposed to the

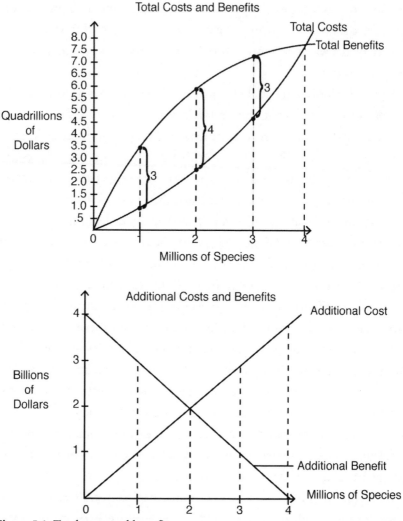

Figure 5.1. Total costs and benefits.

additional benefit from preserving one more, appears in figure 5.1B. (Note that these graphs are fictional representations for the purpose of illustration.) According to these graphs, for example, the cost of preserving the 1 millionth species is $1 billion, the benefit from preserving that species is $3 billion, the total benefit from preserving 1 million species is $3.5 quadrillion, and the total cost is $0.5 quadrillion.

Assuming that our goal is to maximize the net gain from biodiversity, the optimal outcome occurs where the total benefits exceed the total costs by the largest amount. This is the case when 2 million species are preserved and the difference between total benefits and total costs is $4 quadrillion. This optimal number of species is found at the intersection of the additional cost and additional benefit lines. There is good logic behind this convenient benchmark. If the additional benefit from preserving another species exceeds the additional cost, which is true to the left of the intersection of the two lines, then preserving that species will add to the net benefit to society. If the additional benefit from preserving another species is less than the additional cost, as is the case to the right of the intersection, then preserving that species will detract from the net benefit to society. If these costs and benefits are all-inclusive, we maximize social welfare by preserving species until the additional benefit equals the additional cost.

THE NOAH'S ARK MODEL

Metrick and Weitzman (1998) and Weitzman (1998) view the decision of which species to preserve as the "Noah's Ark problem." Like Noah, we have some control over what species can survive on the "ark" we call the earth. There is a cost associated with efforts to preserve species, exemplified by the expense of conservation projects and the forgone profits that could be earned if the species' habitats were not preserved. The value of a species in the Noah's Ark model is measured in terms of direct benefits (commercial, recreational, and emotional) and contributions to diversity (distinctiveness in comparison to the closest relative). The task of prioritizing species for protection—selecting those that can board the ark given limits of space, time, or money—also involves a fourth variable: the increased likelihood of survival attributed to protection. Some species will persist regardless of intervention; others are very vulnerable but can survive with assistance.

Allowing D to represent the value of a species' distinctiveness, B to represent the value of its direct benefits, S to represent the percentage increase in survivability resulting from protection, and C to represent the cost of preservation efforts, the societal gain per dollar expended is $(D + B)(S/C)$. The welfare of society is maximized by prioritizing assistance to those species that provide the greatest additional benefits per dollar's worth of protection and continuing conservation efforts until the additional benefit from one more unit of effort is less than or equal to the cost. To the extent that the values of D, B, S, and C can be estimated, the Noah's Ark model can guide the appropriate prioritization of conservation efforts. Even if the numbers cannot be closely estimated, the model is useful in highlighting the variables and formula policymakers should consider to the extent possible. The following section explains methods for estimating costs and benefits, and the later section on findings discusses several applications of these methods.

VALUING COSTS AND BENEFITS

The central role of cost-benefit analysis in determining appropriate levels of biodiversity warrants a further breakdown of the valuation process. An **indirect valuation** of environmental impacts uses nonmonetary units to measure effects on productivity, health, the environment, and man-made resources. Many of the methods of determining direct valuations as described in this chapter require that individuals understand the costs and benefits of the studied resources or events. When this is not the case, an indirect valuation method can determine the physical loss, and this information can be coupled with dollar values per unit of loss, often obtained using direct valuation methods. For example, if individuals do not understand that trees provide oxygen for them to breathe, direct survey methods are unlikely to reveal the true cost of deforestation and its causes. An indirect valuation might involve measuring the loss of trees and oxygen per acre of land cleared for cattle grazing and multiplying it by the directly revealed value of clean air and forested land to get a better picture of the cost of deforestation.

Direct valuation techniques evaluate the monetary values individuals place on the benefits and costs of biodiversity. Both the existence of a species and the alternatives forgone to preserve the species offer values to users and nonusers alike. **Use values** derive from the firsthand enjoyment of resources and their by-products. While users of forests, for example, benefit from the fresh air and pleasant surroundings, there are others who never enter a forest or see a particular animal species but place a nonuse or **passive-use value** on them. Passive-use values can be divided into **option values** that people place on the option to, say, visit the forest in the future and **existence values** that are unrelated to any possibility of ever using the resource or its by-products. Existence values include **bequest values** from knowing that preservation allows others to use a resource and **sympathy values** from knowing that a resource is alive and well. Evidence of bequest values includes the work of "Johnny Appleseed" and current incarnations. Like planting tree seedlings, recycling efforts may also provide the lion's share of their benefits to future generations. The establishment of nature preserves with no human access is likely to be driven by sympathy values. In practice, our motives for preservation are typically a combination of such interests.

Direct valuation methods explicitly seek monetary values for environmental assets. Values are often measured in terms of people's stated or implied willingness to pay or willingness to accept payment for a resource. An individual's **willingness to pay** is the largest amount of money she or he would be willing to pay in exchange for the resource. An individual's **willingness to accept** is the smallest amount of money she or he would accept to forgo a resource. Note that willingness to accept is determined from the standpoint of already having the resource, and willingness to pay is determined from the standpoint of lacking the resource. Since positions of greater wealth (having versus not having the resource) normally lead individuals to place higher valuations on goods they desire, we can expect the willingness to accept for a given resource to be larger than the willingness to pay.

There are several direct valuation techniques with contrasting strengths and weaknesses. The **contingent valuation** method uses sophisticated surveys to summon revealing responses about the value of resources to society.

To estimate the value people place on forests, clean air, or particular animal species, this approach is simply to ask them. Contingent valuation surveys are valued for their flexibility. They can be customized to collect data on natural resources that have no established market price and whose values would be hard to pinpoint using any other method. This is an advantage over other methods that rely on related travel or purchases, which may not exist for worms, mosses, and the like. The problem with contingent valuation techniques is that those taking the surveys do not actually pay or receive the amounts of money they assign to resources. Saying you would pay $100 to save the banana slug is easier than actually reaching into your pocket and handing over the money. For this reason, survey designers must word questions carefully to encourage a mind-set similar to that which would exist if the money discussed were real.

The **hedonic pricing approach** evaluates differences in the prices of goods or services caused by (in this context) environmental assets or liabilities. If workers are willing to accept a lower wage for planting trees in a forest than for planting seeds on a farm, other things being equal, the difference in accepted wages reflects the workers' valuation of being in the forest and helping to preserve wildlife. Likewise, if the price for similar housing is higher in areas with more biodiversity than in areas with less, other things being equal, this difference reflects a use value for biodiversity. A method called **regression analysis** allows economists to study the effects of chosen variables, such as pollution or biodiversity levels, on prices while holding the effects of all other measurable determinants of prices constant. One drawback of the hedonic pricing approach is that it can be difficult to identify or collect data on all the significant determinants of a product's price. In addition, there are often passive-use values that do not enter into the prices of products connected with the environmental resource. For example, the effect of a wildlife preserve on housing prices in one area does not indicate the existence or option values of that preserve for people living in other areas.

In some cases, market prices contribute to the estimation of biodiversity valuations. The market prices of health products, food, travel, and so on attributable to biodiversity indicate the minimum valuation current users place on those products and services. That is, rational buyers would not pay more for a product than what it is worth to them. For example, we can learn about the use value of rain forests by considering the time, travel costs, and entry fees spent in order to see them and the prices people pay for medicines, dyes, and fruits taken from them. Of course, some users would pay more than the market price for the products they consume, meaning that valuations based on market prices are conservative unless they account for the value in excess of the market price (as could be estimated, for example, with a contingent valuation survey). According to economic theory, in a market with sufficient competition among firms, information about prices and products, and **internalization** of outcomes (the decisions of consumers and producers affect only the decision makers), the price of a good also reflects the cost of producing one more unit of that good. Thus, the price of a good can be used to approximate both the costs and the benefits associated with the last unit of that good. Major exceptions are discussed later in the section on market failure.

Biodiversity loss involves the complicating factors of uncertainty and irreversibility. We never know what benefits would have come from a lost species or how many species are eliminated before being discovered, but the benefits attained from existing species and the measured decline in known species give us some indication. According to Taylor (1998), 121 prescription drugs are currently derived from plants, and a quarter of all Western pharmaceuticals are derived from rain forest ingredients, while only 1 in 100 plants has been tested for medicinal value. Some estimate that thousands or tens of thousands of species are lost each year (Myers 1981; Taylor 1998).

Even when the virtues of a species are known, extinction lasts forever, and the valuation of annual losses must be extended into the future. If we valued future costs and benefits the same as today's, any positive yearly value would become infinite when multiplied by the infinite number of years ahead. Economic models generally presume that we discount the value of future benefits in some way, meaning that a dollar's worth of benefits realized a year from now is worth less than a dollar today and that a dollar's worth of benefits realized 100 years from now is worth much less yet.

The next dilemma is what discount rate to place on future benefits and costs. The interest rate on loans is one available guide, being the compensation lenders receive for putting off the use of each dollar for another year. For example, if an interest rate of 5% (or, equivalently, 0.05) is used to estimate the discount we place on a dollar's worth of benefits received next year, then the value we place today on receiving a dollar's worth of benefits next year is $1/(1 + 0.05)$, or $0.9524. Similarly, the value we place today on receiving a dollar's worth of benefits in 100 years is $1/(1 + 0.05)^{100}$, or $0.0076. With d representing the discount rate and n representing the number of years in the future, the formula $1/(1 + d)^n$ can be used to evaluate the present value of future costs as well as benefits.[1]

MARKET FAILURE

This section begins with an explanation of how a market can work efficiently and then explains potential pitfalls. The standard graphical model of a market appears in figure 5.2. The **demand curve** shows the relationship between price and the quantity demanded of a good or service within a given period. For example, based on figure 5.2, Austin would purchase 12 Brazil nuts at a price of 10 cents each and 4 at a price of 25 cents each. An individual's demand curve for a good reflects the additional benefit (measured in dollars) received from each incremental unit of the good consumed. Austin values the first Brazil nut at $0.35, the second at $0.32, and so on. A line through the points on this graph constitutes a demand curve. Notice that Austin receives less and less additional benefit per nut as he purchases more and more nuts. This makes sense. His first Brazil nut will go toward his greatest need, perhaps extreme hunger. As he consumes more nuts, he becomes less hungry, and his nuts are used to satisfy less and less important needs (feeding squirrels, throwing at signposts, and so on).

The **supply curve** for a producer shows the relationship between price and quantity supplied by that producer within a given period. As the price

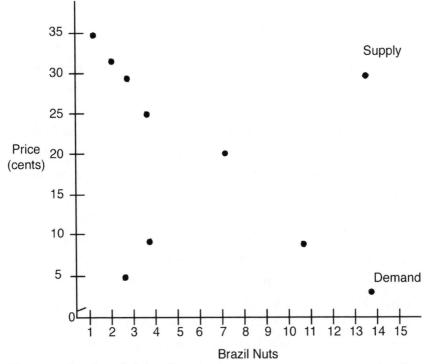

Figure 5.2. Supply-and-demand curve.

increases, the quantity of a good supplied in a given period will increase, other things being equal. Think about how many Brazil nuts a producer would be willing to supply at different prices. At a price of 5 cents, she probably would not be very enthused about the prospects but perhaps would be willing to give up some of her least valuable time—that otherwise spent watching golf on television—to collect a handful of Brazil nuts. With such a low return, she might not want to give up your second-least-favorite pastime of watching game shows in order to collect more nuts. However, if the price rose to 30 cents per Brazil nut, forget *The Price Is Right*—she might be willing to spend more time and invest more money into collecting 15 Brazil nuts. Just as the value of lost opportunities increases as one spends more and more time collecting nuts, other cost components are likely to increase as well. For more nuts, she will have to go after those farther from reach. At some point, she might need to hire help and then pay them overtime and so on. All this results in a supply curve that slopes upward, meaning that more will be produced only for a higher price.

The demand curve and the supply curve for a particular good live on the same graph, with price on the horizontal axis and quantity on the vertical axis. Since the additional benefit from the first few units of a good is often relatively high and the additional cost of producing the first few units often relatively low (as explained previously), the demand curve begins above the supply curve as in figure 5.2. The point of intersection between the two curves is called the **equilibrium** point. Assume for simplicity that Austin is the only consumer of Brazil nuts and that you are the only supplier. It is only at the equilibrium price of $0.20 that the quantity of Brazil nuts demanded equals the quantity supplied. If the price were above $0.20, say $0.30, the 15 Brazil nuts supplied would exceed the 3 demanded. The resulting surplus of 12 Brazil nuts would lead you, as producer, to lower your price until equilibrium was reached. Likewise, if the price were below $0.20, say $0.10, a shortage of 8 Brazil nuts would exist because the 12 demanded would exceed the 4 supplied. With a line out your door of people wanting to purchase Brazil nuts, it would make sense to raise your price until the quantity demanded equaled the quantity you wanted to supply at the current price, which occurs at equilibrium. In the long run, economic theory predicts that the market price and quantity will equal the equilibrium price and quantity.

Since the supply curve reflects the cost of production and the demand curve reflects the benefits to consumers of the good, there is a wonderfully convenient result at equilibrium—the costs and benefits from one more unit of the good are equalized. The previous section on cost-benefit analysis explains why resources are allocated efficiently when activities including the production of goods and services continue until the additional cost equals the additional benefit. Eighteenth-century economist and philosopher Adam Smith noted that under ideal circumstances, the market achieves this goal with little intervention, as if guided by an invisible hand. Unfortunately, the market might fail in a number of ways, and biodiversity is especially vulnerable to several common types of market failure.

Market failure and an associated misallocation of resources, such as overproduction of a good or service, can result from imperfect competition, imperfect information, externalities, or public goods. The problem of **imperfect competition** occurs when sellers have sufficient market power to charge unnecessarily high prices, limit the quantity produced, or produce goods of inferior quality. Each of these practices leads to an inefficient allocation of resources that does not equate the additional costs and benefits of production. The Federal Trade Commission (FTC) was created in 1914 to detect and punish unfair methods of competition as well as unfair or deceptive business practices. Although the FTC is effective in many circumstances, it does not have the ability to prevent all abuses of market power.

The problem of **imperfect information** exists when buyers or sellers do not have adequate knowledge about available markets, prices, products, customers, suppliers, and so forth. This can lead, for example, to buyers paying too much for a product because they do not know about a lower-priced alternative or producers making too much of one thing and not enough of another because they do not understand the desires of their customers. Solutions to imperfect information include truth-in-advertising regulations, consumer information services, and market surveys by firms.

Externalities are costs or benefits felt beyond or "external to" those causing the effects. Inefficiencies arise out of these spillover effects because decision makers do not consider all the repercussions of their behavior. Producers, for example, are unlikely to consider the costs imposed by pollution from their factories when deciding how much to produce. If the pollution causes losses to biodiversity and health that are not considered in the production decisions, producers will produce too much. Likewise, tropical rain forests offer the makings of future medicinal cures. If the value of these cures is not considered when weighing the costs and benefits of deforestation, too many rain forest acres will be cleared.

There are several solutions to problems with externalities. The socially optimal resource allocation can be achieved if the private costs and benefits felt by decision makers are equated with the costs and benefits to society. Activities that cause negative externalities, such as deforestation, can be taxed by the amount of the spillover effect, causing the development companies to feel or "internalize" the full costs of their behavior. Likewise, activities causing positive externalities, such as education and the planting of seedlings, can be subsidized by the value of the spillover effect so that the private benefits to students and seedling planters equal the benefits to society. This is why, for example, Jimmy Carter advocated subsidies for users of solar panels and at the same time taxes on gasoline.

Ronald Coase (1960) suggested that those who are helped or hurt by externalities might be able to pay the decision makers to produce more or less of their product. The success of such payoffs is contingent on the clarity of each side's rights under law and the ability of the affected parties to organize together and collect the necessary funds. Suppose a factory receives $10,000 worth of benefits from dumping effluent into a stream, that this dumping eliminates a species of fish from the stream, and that the factory has a clearly defined right to do the dumping. If the neighboring town receives $20,000 worth of benefits from the presence of the fish, Coase predicts the town would pay the factory some amount between $10,000 and $20,000 not to pollute, thus making both sides better off than with the dumping. With a payment of $15,000 from the town to the factory, for example, the factory receives $5,000 more than its $10,000 gain from dumping, and the town loses $5,000 less than the alternative $20,000 loss due to dumping. Unfortunately, biodiversity loss affects large numbers of people around the world, and it is often prohibitively difficult for the affected parties to be identified and work together in negotiations. Alternative solutions for negative externalities include regulations that restrict the quantity of output to the socially optimal level or taxes that bring the producers' costs per unit up to the full costs to society.

Public goods are those that many individuals benefit from at the same time. They are characterized as being nonrival in consumption and nonexcludable. For a good to be nonrival means that one person's consumption of that good does not affect its consumption by others. This is common for animal species that are appreciated for their existence value—my enjoyment of the fact that pandas still roam in China does not affect your enjoyment of the same thing. Multiple users, on the other hand, cannot consume **rival goods**, such as food and parking spaces, at the same time. Once available, nonexcludable goods cannot be held back from those who desire access. For example, if the trend of global warming is stabilized or reversed, it is impossible to prevent particular individuals from benefiting from that turnaround. Other examples of public goods include police protection, disease control, clean air, and the preservation of natural resources.

Since multiple users benefit from a public good at the same time, the value to society of each additional unit of the good is found by adding together the values to each individual. That is, if there are 10 people on an island and each places a $1,000 value on the existence of the first bald eagle on that island, the value of the first bald eagle to this small society is $10,000. They should be willing to pay up to $10,000 to preserve habitat for the first eagle. The problem with public goods is that individuals know they can benefit from the existence of these goods whether or not they pay for them. Even if each person gains $1,000 worth of enjoyment from the eagle, a door-to-door collection to pay for its preservation would come up short because of the temptation for individuals to be **free riders**. A free rider is one who attempts to benefit from a public good without paying for it. Given the nonrival and nonexcludable nature of many natural resources, individuals have little incentive to reveal their true preferences for them. Instead, they will deny interest and then benefit from the preservation efforts of others. A solution to the free rider problem is to have the government provide public goods and pay for them with taxes collected from everyone who stands to benefit from the public goods. This is how many of our parks and wildlife preservation efforts are funded today.

Findings

Metrick and Weitzman (1998) have collected data to examine the selection of species for preservation based on the four criteria of the Noah's Ark model explained previously—direct benefits, distinctiveness, survivability, and cost. For measures of society's rankings of species, they looked to the nomination process for protection under the Endangered Species Act. This included counts of positive comments made about species, the decision whether to include species on the protected list, and the amounts of public expenditures on the recovery of species. Direct benefits were measured in terms of species' size and taxonomic class, the most popular of which they called "charismatic megafauna." As a measure of distinctiveness, they determined whether a species was the sole representative of its genus and whether it was a subspecies. For survivability, they used a 1–5 ranking of endangerment created by The Nature Conservancy, and for cost they used a variable indicating whether recovery of the species conflicts with public or private development plans.

Metrick and Weitzman's findings indicate that we place a high priority on the large, cuddly "charismatic megafauna." More surprisingly, their findings suggest that society spends more money on less endangered species than on more endangered species, and it does not increase spending significantly for more unique species. Further, we are more likely to spend money on an animal whose preservation conflicts with development plans than on those that could be saved at a lower cost. In other words, our current strategies for environmental protection do not coincide with what most economists would recommend in terms of maximizing social welfare.

A number of studies have placed specific values on various species. W. Kip Viscusi (1993) reports on 30 studies of the value of human life. On the average, these studies suggest that *Homo sapiens* value their lives at about $8 million a piece (this and all figures are adjusted for inflation using the consumer price index to reflect year 2000 dollars). The hedonic pricing method was prevalent among these studies of the value of human life. For example, some investigators measured trade-offs between wages and risks of occupational fatalities, correcting for other determinants of wages. If the average worker will accept an extra $800 per year in exchange for a 1 in 10,000 annual risk of death, that worker implicitly values 1/10,000 of his or her life at $800, and an entire life would be worth 10,000 × $800 = $8,000,000. Other observable trade-offs between risks of death and money or time (which has monetary value) involve driving speeds, the purchase of safety equipment, and safety belt use.

Several contingent valuation surveys have elicited individuals' willingness to pay to preserve animal species. Reaves et al. (1999) asked individuals what they would pay per year to increase the probability of survival of the red-cockaded woodpecker from 50% to 99%. The average willingness to pay was about $14, which would indicate a preservation value of $3.8 billion per year to the 274 million U.S. residents. Bowker and Stoll (1988) and Stevens et al. (1991) used similar contingent valuation surveys to estimate per-person per-year values of $45 and $35 for whooping cranes and bald eagles, respectively. The corresponding values for all U.S. residents are $12.3 billion and $9.6 billion. Looking into the future with a 5% discount factor per year, the total present values would be $76 billion for red-cockaded woodpeckers, $246 billion for whooping cranes, and $192 billion for bald eagles. In each case, the estimated values were for the protection of a single species. As explained previously, as more and more species are eliminated, the value of protecting subsequent species is expected to increase.

Rubin et al. (1991) used contingent valuation methods to estimate a value for the spotted owl of about $43 per resident of Washington State. They went on to calculate the cost of preservation in terms of logging jobs and effects on the price of timber. The long-term gains from preservation turned out to be $1.84 million, while the long-term costs were $0.62 million. Given that benefits exceed costs, the appropriate policy would be to preserve the species. If logging were to continue, Coase would point out that both those benefiting from preservation and those harmed by it would be better off if those harmed were compensated with any amount between $0.62 million and $1.84 million in exchange for preservation. If those in the timber market were compensated with exactly their $0.62 loss, society at large would gain $1.84 − $0.62 = $1.22 million relative to its position with logging.

The additional economic literature on the valuation of biodiversity is vast and global. Adrian Phillips (1998) of the World Commission on Protected Areas provides the following estimates from case studies: Forests in Kenya are worth $323 per household per year for medicines, wild foods, hunting, building materials, and the like. The total present value of Borivli National Park to residents in Bombay is $35 million. The introduction of lion into the Pilanesberg Protected Area in South Africa cost between $74,000 and $784,000 for purchase and maintenance but increased tourism revenues by between $6.2 million and $14 million. And in Nepal, broadleaf forests have a net present value between $2,877 and $3,807 per hectare (a hectare equals 2.47 acres), while evergreen forests in the same region are valued at $2,282 per hectare. The important point is that we are not in the dark when it comes to the valuation of nonmarket goods. Increasingly thorough and accurate estimates based on a variety of techniques are available to guide efficient policymaking.

Conclusions

The tools of economics lend themselves naturally to the valuation and management of biodiversity. Economic theory suggests that resources are not allocated efficiently by a free market in the face of imperfect information, imperfect competition, or spillover effects felt beyond those causing the effects. In these cases of market failure, intervention can improve or worsen the outcome, depending on its administration. It is in society's best interest to prioritize conservation efforts on the basis of their broadly defined return per unit of expenditure and carry out those projects for which the return equals or exceeds the cost. The appropriate management of biodiversity must rest on carefully considered values that are direct and indirect, present and future, financial and emotional, and well informed. Only then can we make wise trade-offs between natural resources and the competing fruits of civilization.

N O T E

1. The proof of these formulas is beyond the scope of this chapter, but further discussion is available in most economics textbooks under the topic of present-value calculations.

REFERENCES

Bowker, J. M., and J. R. Stoll. 1988. Use of dichotomous choice nonmarket methods to value the whooping crane resource. *American Journal of Agricultural Economics* 70:372–81.

Coase, Ronald H. 1960. The problem of social cost. *Journal of Law and Economics* 3(2):1–45.

Metrick, Andrew, and Martin L. Weitzman. 1998. Conflicts and choices in biodiversity. *Journal of Economic Perspectives* 12(3):21–34.

Myers, Norman. 1981. The exhausted earth. *Foreign Policy* 42(1):141–55.

Phillips, Adrian. 1998. Economic values of protected areas: Guidelines for protected area managers. Cambridge, U.K.: IUCN Publications Services Unit.

Reaves D. W., R. A. Kramer, and T. P. Holmes. 1999. Does question format matter? Valuing an endangered species. *Environmental and Resource Economics* 14(3):365–83.

Rubin, Jonathan, Gloria Helfand, and John Loomis. 1991. A benefit-cost analysis of the northern spotted owl. *Journal of Forestry Research* 89:25–30.

Stevens, T. H., J. Echeverria, R. J. Glass, T. Hager, and T. A. Moore. 1991. Measuring the existence value of wildlife: What do CVM estimates really show? *Land Economics* 67:390–400.

Taylor, Leslie. 1998. Herbal secrets of the rainforest. Roseville, Calif.: Prima.

Viscusi, W. Kip. 1993. The value of risks to life and health. *Journal of Economic Literature* 31(4):1912–46.

Weitzman, Martin L. 1998. The Noah's Ark problem. *Econometrica* 66(6):1279–98.

SUGGESTED READINGS

Bateman, I., D. Pearce, and R. K. Turner. 1993. *Environmental economics: An elementary introduction.* Baltimore: The Johns Hopkins University Press.

Brown, G. M., Jr., and R. Rowthorn. 1995. *The economics and ecology of biodiversity decline.* Cambridge: Cambridge University Press.

Costanza, Robert, ed. 1991. *Ecological economics: The science and management of sustainability.* New York: Columbia University Press.

Dodds, D. E., J. A. Lesser, and R. O. Zerbe, Jr. 1997. *Environmental economics and policy.* New York: Addison-Wesley Longman.

Field, Barry C. 1997. *Environmental economics: An introduction.* Boston: Irwin McGraw-Hill.

Flint, M. 1992. Biological diversity and developing countries. In *Environmental economics: A reader.* Edited by A. Markandya and J. Richardson. New York: St. Martin's, 437–69.

Goodstein, E. S. 1999. *Economics and the environment.* Englewood Cliffs, N.J.: Prentice Hall.

Gowdy, J. M., and C. N. McDaniel. 1995. One world, one experiment: Addressing the biodiversity-economics conflict. *Ecological Economics* 15(2):165–78.

Kahn, J. R. 1998. *The economic approach to environmental and natural resources.* Orlando: Dryden.

Klemperer, D. W. 1996. *Forest resource economics and finance.* New York: McGraw-Hill.

Mann, C. C., and M. L. Plummer. 1993. The high cost of biodiversity. *Science* 260:1868–71.

Marggraf, R., and R. Birner. 1998. The conservation of biological diversity from an economic point of view. *Theory in Biosciences* 117(3):289–306.

Pearce, D., and D. Moran. 1994. *The economics of biodiversity.* London: Earthscan.

Special Issue on the Economics of Biodiversity Loss. 1992. *Ambio* 21(3).

Sterner, T., ed. 1994. *Economic policies for sustainable development.* Amsterdam: Kluwer.

Swanson, Timothy, ed. 1995. *The economics and ecology of biodiversity decline.* Cambridge: Cambridge University Press.

Swerdlow, Joel L. 1999. Biodiversity. *National Geographic,* February, 6–8.

Symposium on the Endangered Species Act. 1998. *Journal of Economic Perspectives* 12(3):3–52.

Tietenberg, T. 1992. *Environmental and natural resource economics.* New York: HarperCollins.

———. 1998. *Environmental economics and policy.* New York: Addison-Wesley Longman.

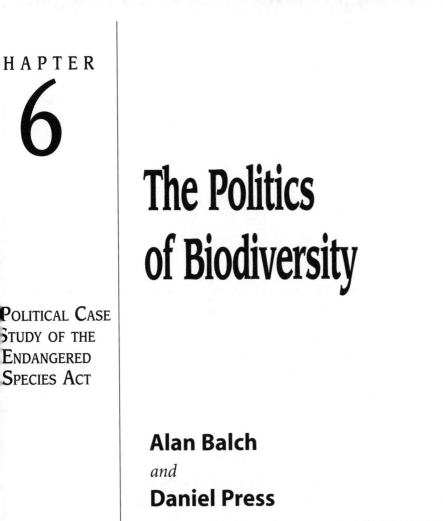

6

The Politics of Biodiversity

POLITICAL CASE
STUDY OF THE
ENDANGERED
SPECIES ACT

Alan Balch
and
Daniel Press

The natural sciences generate powerful arguments for biodiversity's ecological importance, provide strong evidence of its alarmingly rapid decline, and identify possible methods for its protection (see Wilson 2002) However, creating institutions capable of protecting biodiversity is largely a political endeavor. The **politics** and **policies** of species protection are therefore an essential part of understanding the biodiversity dilemma.

In this chapter, we review the U.S. political experience with biodiversity, with special emphasis on the Endangered Species Act (ESA) of 1973. We focus on the United States because it contains an enormous amount of biodiversity under severe threat of extinction and because the United States has been implementing the world's most stringent biodiversity protection law for nearly three decades.

Policymaking in the United States

At the federal, state, and local levels, the American political system is designed to provide a series of checks and balances through divided government. Political power is separated among the **legislative**, **executive**, and **judicial** branches, each with ability to oversee the other and each with different constituencies, term limits, and sanctioning powers. Authority is further fragmented within each particular branch. For example, the executive branch consists of many departments and agencies, each of which is designed to handle different issues. The fact that political power is separated between different branches and then fragmented within those branches has significant implications for policymaking and change, as the ESA's political story will demonstrate.

To help make sense of the seemingly chaotic politics, events, and actions driving policy creation and change, political scientists often employ a simplistic model of the policy process, broken down into discrete stages (Lester and Stewart 1996):

$$\text{Agenda Setting} \rightarrow \text{Enactment} \rightarrow \text{Implementation} \rightarrow$$
$$\text{Modification} \rightarrow \text{Termination}$$

Our model's first stage, agenda setting, is based on John Kingdon's (1995) work. In stage I, three factors—problems, politics, and policy alternatives—interact to open windows of opportunity for new or renewed efforts at addressing social issues. Some problems become salient over time, following years of education or effort on the part of political actors, while others burst onto the scene following a "focusing event" (such as the *Exxon Valdez* oil spill). Once a problem becomes salient, political struggles ensue over the problem's causes and the placement of blame. This "political story" strongly affects the attention a problem receives and the policy alternatives that emerge as solutions. A multitude of political events, such as elections, hearings, campaigns, speeches, and national mood swings, provide opportunities for political actors to define problems, cast blame, push specific solutions, and pursue other agendas.

Most problems never move past the agenda-setting stage because they fall from the public spotlight, no one can agree on a feasible solution, political opportunities are missed, or any combination thereof. Alternatively, a problem is most likely to move into stage II, **policy enactment**, when significant attention, feasible policy prescriptions, and political opportunities combine to open "policy windows" (Kingdon 1995).

Once a policy has been enacted, attention to the problem may wane because people believe that the recently enacted legislation will now address the problem. Anthony Downs (1972) refers to this phenomenon as an "issue attention cycle," wherein a problem receives significant attention, a law is passed, and then public interest drops or shifts to other issues. However, a policy will not solve the problem it was designed to address unless it is implemented (stage III).

Primarily the function of executive departments and agencies (such as the U.S. Fish and Wildlife Service), implementation requires resources such as staff and money. It may also require new programs and policies, especially when the **enabling statute** contains lofty goals and time lines without detailed instructions on how to achieve policy goals and/or political situations unforeseen by lawmakers (Mazmanian and Sabatier 1989). In such cases, the implementing executive agency often creates additional rules, referred to as regulations, that carry the same power as law and in effect that constitute new policies.

Ideally, a statute and its regulations would be completely and successfully implemented and the problem remedied. This circumstance, however, is rare. According to Mazmanian and Sabatier (1989), the **implementation** process is affected by numerous variables, including the capacity of implementing officials, the clarity of a statute, and the level of behavioral change targeted by the statute. As we will demonstrate through the ESA's political history, those in opposition to a particular policy often try to block implementation by filing lawsuits, not cooperating with agency officials, finding statutory loopholes, or lobbying Congress to weaken or repeal the law. The legislative branch can also impede or alter implementation over time by underfunding the policy or making changes to it. Alternatively, those who feel that the policy is being improperly implemented may also file lawsuits or lobby Congress to strengthen the statute.

Sometime during the course of implementation—often repeatedly—the policy is evaluated. Our definition of evaluation encompasses 1) legal evaluations of the statute's authority or the actions of implementing officials that must be settled in court, 2) political evaluations of the statute's impact that may occur in congressional committees (such as **oversight hearings**) or the implementing agency itself, and 3) and social evaluations that often occur in the media. Policies are often evaluated in several of these arenas at once. As we will see in the ESA's case, evaluations are often motivated by other issues (such as property rights) rising and falling on the political agenda that conflict with or attempt to override established policy.

Evaluations often lead to policy changes (stage IV). Modifications can range from incremental to extensive, and the rate of change may vary from slow to rapid. Baumgartner and Jones (1993) argue that incrementalism is the norm in politics because when a policy is created, institutions develop around that policy (such as staff, research, regulations, and money), allowing privileged access to supporters. These institutions will work diligently to perpetuate their survival, which at times may mean incremental policy change to improve policy performance and/or silence criticism. However, Baumgartner and Jones also assert that periods of incrementalism are often punctuated by extensive and swift policy change following successful efforts by policy opponents to convey a negative image of the policy in a venue or institution more apt to side with their negative assessment. By redefining a policy's image (such as arguing that species protection results in job losses) and/or drawing attention to a competing image (such as that property rights should not be restricted in order to protect species) while simultaneously instigating evaluations of the issue in a different venue (such as the courts or a congressional committee), opponents can often attract new participants and generate some political momentum that may result in significant policy departures.

Opportunities to push both incremental and extensive policy revisions are quite frequent because the U.S. political system is designed for constant policy evaluations and modifications. Each branch of government has the power to oversee the political actions of another. Moreover, many policies have set authorization periods after which lawmakers must consider whether to reauthorize them for another period. When a bill is up for reauthorization (as the ESA has been numerous times), Congress often holds hearings to assess the statute. A new law must be passed to extend the previous one's authority, and this offers opportunities to make statutory changes or kill the act entirely. Even if reauthorization efforts fail, Congress can keep the law alive through continued appropriations (this has been true in the ESA's case since 1993).

The final stage is policy termination. A policy may be designed to expire after a certain length of time. Alternatively, a policy's demise may be politically orchestrated because it is thought to be too expensive or ineffective, new policies are enacted to replace the old, or the problem that a policy was designed to address is corrected (Lester and Stewart 1996). Although all issues must endure this complicated process if they are to be corrected politically, some problems are inherently more amenable to political remedies than others.

Mazmanian and Sabatier (1989) argue that an issue's "tractability" often determines its political fate. A highly tractable problem is one that is technically simple, is caused by a single behavior, and is relatively inexpensive to address. In addition, a tractable problem requires a degree of certainty that modest changes in behavior by a target group will solve the problem (Mazmanian and Sabatier 1989).

In addition to a problem's tractability, the costs and benefits associated with its policy prescriptions are critical determinants of political struggles (Wilson 1980). It is politically advantageous to show that a policy's social, moral, and/or financial benefits outweigh the costs. James Wilson (1980) contends that a policy solution is likely to garner little political support if the perceived or actual costs are high, immediate, and concentrated on small groups while the perceived or actual benefits are low, slow in coming, and diffused among several groups.

Of course, the characteristics of a problem and possible solutions are the "stuff" of political battles. Those who advocate action to address some problem will often try to convince the public and elected officials that critical damage is being inflicted by a private or public group, a simple cause-and-effect relationship exists, solving the problem is relatively simple or absolutely necessary, and the benefits outweigh the costs. Opponents will make a contrary case. Such debate clouds the political waters, especially for issues that are inherently complicated, like biodiversity protection.

Biodiversity as a Political Problem

"Over the past two decades, the protection of biological diversity has emerged as one of the most significant and controversial areas of environmental law and policy" (Menell and Stewart 1994, 1130). This issue is challenging in part because of a politically weak causal story and low tractability. The blame for biodiversity loss is often difficult to ascribe to one source, while the scientific arguments for the importance of biodiversity can be highly complex; many citizens and elected officials probably do not understand what biodiversity is and why it is important. Furthermore, the causes of biodiversity loss can be traced to a variety of common actions and actors (such as development, logging, pollution, farming, and wetlands conversion), meaning that the behavioral changes and the number of people affected are potentially extensive if the political goal is large-scale biodiversity protection.

The social and ecological benefits derived from protecting biodiversity are rarely immediate or tangible and are dispersed throughout society as they accrue over time (Tobin 1990). Moreover, the only way to protect biodiversity is through habitat preservation (National Research Council 1995), which can be expensive and may conflict with other powerful political values, such as economic growth and property rights. Industry and landowners are quick to produce dollar figures estimating the economic losses imposed by restrictions on property and/or resource uses. However, measuring the benefits of biodiversity preservation in dollars is usually impossible, and the ecological benefits of doing so are often difficult to prove, difficult to measure, and difficult to comprehend (Tobin 1990). Because financial benefits and costs are typically easiest to measure and often take precedence within the walls of government, biodiversity policy can be politically problematic. Given these various political challenges, it is remarkable that the United States has such a strong biodiversity law on the books and that this statute has survived relatively intact since 1973.

An Introduction to the Endangered Species Act

The Endangered Species Act (16 U.S. Code §1531 et seq.) is a comprehensive statute designed to protect both endangered and threatened species in addition to the ecosystems on which such species depend (§1531 b). In stating its rationale for the ESA, Congress declared that economic growth and development, without concern for conservation, was responsible for the disappearance of various species of fish, wildlife, and plants in the United States. Such species, according to Congress, deserve protection because of their "aesthetic, ecological, educational, historical, recreational and scientific value to the Nation and its people" (§1531 a).

The act defines an endangered species as one in danger of extinction throughout all or a significant portion of its range. An organism that is likely to become an endangered species within the foreseeable future is classified as threatened. Most species are considered for listing under the act on the basis of a petition process that allows private entities to submit a formal listing request for a species. The secretary of the interior or in some cases the secretary of commerce is charged with determining whether to list a species as threatened or endangered, a decision that must be based on the best scientific and commercial data available without regard to economic or other impacts.

Concurrent with listing, the appropriate secretary designates the listed species' critical habitat—the geographic areas that include the biological or physical features essential to the conservation of the species. Designation of critical habitat must be based on the best scientific data available, but economic and other relevant impacts also must be considered when specifying critical habitat. The secretary is also required to develop and implement recovery plans that delineate management actions necessary for a species' resurgence and its eventual removal from the list.

A listed species and its habitat are afforded significant protection under ESA provisions. Public and private entities are prohibited from "taking" an endangered species, which is defined in the statute as to "harass, harm, pursue, hunt, shoot, wound, kill, trap, capture, or collect" (§1532 19). In 1975, the agency primarily responsible for implementing the ESA, the U.S. Fish and Wildlife Service (FWS), issued regulations defining "harm" as any action resulting in habitat modification that jeopardized a listed species' existence (50 CFR §17.3).

The act has additional provisions to ensure that species will not be harmed by federal actions. If a listed species or critical habitat is likely to be affected by a federal agency's actions, then that agency must consult with the FWS. During consultation, the agency involved submits a biological assessment to the secretary identifying any listed species that may be affected. The secretary subsequently files a biological opinion of this assessment. An agency is clear to proceed if the secretary's opinion states that no listed species or critical habitat would be affected. However, if the secretary finds that a listed species or its critical habitat is in jeopardy, then a written statement is issued, suggesting any reasonable and prudent alternatives to the proposed action.

Private citizens also are forbidden to take a listed species. However, they can file for a permit that allows a "take," provided that such action is incidental to and not the purpose of the implementation of otherwise lawful activity. To receive a permit, a private entity must submit a description of the activity requiring authorization and a highly detailed conservation plan commonly known as a habitat conservation plan. An "incidental take permit" can be issued by the secretary only if it is determined that the applicant will minimize and mitigate the impacts of any incidental takings, that adequate funding exists for the conservation plan, and that the taking will not significantly reduce the species chances for survival and recovery. The ESA also contains some important enforcement provisions, including fines ranging from $500 to $50,000 and prison sentences ranging from six months to a year for those who violate the ESA. Furthermore, "any person" is authorized by the statute to file a suit to enjoin ESA violations.

What follows is a review of the events leading up to the ESA's creation followed by overviews of subsequent political battles concerning the act that eventually became so divisive that Congress has been unable to agree on its scheduled reauthorization for over a decade. This discussion is not designed to provide a detailed account of the ESA and the controversies surrounding it over the years (sources for such information are in the references). Rather, we highlight key political episodes that demonstrate the evolutionary process of policymaking, elucidate the challenges facing biodiversity policy, and provide a sense of the ESA's effectiveness.

The Politics of Policy Creation and Change

The ESA's roots can be traced at least back to 1964, when the Department of the Interior created the Committee on Rare and Endangered Wildlife Species. The nine biologists that made up the committee published the "Redbook"—a document containing the U.S. government's first endangered species list consisting of 63 species (Menell and Stewart 1994). Although species on this list did not receive formal protection, it was the first sign of a nascent national movement calling for attention to vanishing species (Yaffee 1982).

Federal efforts to preserve endangered species soon followed with the Endangered Species Preservation Act of 1966 (Public Law [P.L.] 89-669) signed by President Lyndon Johnson (D) and the Endangered Species Conservation Act of 1969 (P.L. 91-135) signed by President Richard Nixon (R). The 1966 statute charged the secretary of the interior with designating, protecting, and restoring species considered on the brink of extinction (Congressional Quarterly [hereafter CQ] 1966). The 1969 law expanded the previous law by prohibiting the importation and sale of certain endangered species, such as elephants and leopards (Yaffee 1982).

Both the 1966 and 1969 laws were drafted by the Department of the Interior and moved through the House and Senate with minimal debate. Moreover, these early endangered species laws coincided with what numerous scholars contend was a period of heightened ecological consciousness that provided political opportunities to push environmental policy (Vig and Kraft 2000). As the country's environmental awareness grew, so too did the political influence of numerous environmental advocacy groups and the zeal with which many politicians addressed the more popular environmental issues. Water and air quality, along with endangered species, were some of the many issues attracting significant political attention. Socially popular animals close to extinction (such as the Kodiak bear, the California condor, the American alligator, the California gray whale, and the bald eagle) became public symbols of an increasingly salient policy problem (CQ 1966).

The Department of the Interior claimed that the current biodiversity laws were not comprehensive enough and helped launch legislative efforts to extend the provisions of previous legislation beginning in 1970. Although these efforts were unsuccessful, it was obvious that a political window was opening for a comprehensive federal policy. Even President Nixon asserted in his 1972 environmental message that current law "simply [did] not provide the kind of management tools needed to act early enough to save a vanishing species" (CQ 1972). Comprehensive legislation to that effect was introduced in Congress that year. Although the legislation was unsuccessful, it laid much of the groundwork for the landmark 1973 ESA.

President Nixon again called for a more stringent endangered species law in his 1973 environmental message and sent a bill to the Congress that was submitted in both houses (Yaffee 1982). His bill joined several others already introduced in 1973, most of which shared some common themes: species were going extinct, destruction of critical habitat was the most significant threat to species, and an important key to solving this problem was "to protect the ecosystems upon which endangered and threatened species depend" (CQ 1973). It was also clear that the federal government—responsible for managing a full third of the nation's territory—was going to closely regulate its own actions by prohibiting any federal agency from damaging a species or its critical habitat (Congressional Research Service 1982). All these provisions were eventually consolidated into one bill titled the Endangered Species Act.

By a **voice vote** in the Senate and a 355–4 vote in the House, Congress approved the ESA and sent it to President Nixon. On December 28, 1973, Nixon signed the act into law (P.L. 93-205), creating an enormously powerful and comprehensive environmental statute designed to protect biodiversity. A problem (vanishing species), a political trend (a national mood favoring tough environmental policy), and policy solutions (the earlier policy work on numerous species preservation bills) had all converged to open an enormous window through which this impressive legislation passed.

TELLICO DAM

Although it was not obvious to many lawmakers at the time of passage, the ESA's strict guidelines for protecting endangered species provided citizens and environmental groups with a new tool for challenging development, especially if it was being conducted by a federal agency. The events leading up to the most famous example began unfolding at about the same time that the act was being crafted on Capitol Hill.

In 1966, Congress appropriated funds to the Tennessee Valley Authority (TVA) for the construction of the Tellico Dam on the Little Tennessee River (Plater et al. 1992). Local citizens and national conservation groups were concerned about the farmland, recreational opportunities, and sacred Indian grounds that would be lost once the dam closed its gates but were unsuccessful in their various legal and political attempts to permanently stop the project (Bonine and McGarity 1984). A tiny fish, however, was able to turn the tide for the opposition. In 1973, an ichthyologist discovered a previously unknown perch species, the snail darter, in the waters near the project area. The dam's detractors quickly filed a petition with the secretary of the interior to have the species listed as endangered. In October 1975, the secretary formally listed the snail darter as endangered and designated its critical habitat as the same area slated for significant modification by the Tellico Dam (Bonine and McGarity 1984). Consequently, construction on the dam would have to stop because operating it would violate the ESA, but TVA disagreed and continued construction.

Opposition groups filed an ESA-based lawsuit against TVA to stop the project. After losing in federal appellate court, TVA appealed its case to the U.S. Supreme Court in 1978. While presenting his case before the justices, TVA's attorney held up a glass jar containing the snail darter. He asked the Court how a three-inch fish could be valued more highly than a multimillion-dollar dam. Because Congress had declared the value of a species as incalculable, the court found it "difficult . . . to balance the loss of a sum certain—even $100 million—against a congressionally declared incalculable value" (Mennel and Stewart 1994, 1142). Claiming that the act's statutory language and legislative history unequivocally afforded endangered species the highest of priorities in cases such as Tellico, the Court ruled 6–3 in favor of the fish.

Many members of Congress were outraged by the decision. A finished dam that cost $119 million would sit idle because of a fish. Although only one other federal project had been halted by the ESA in five years, accusations that the act had "gone too far" and that "federal protection of wildlife was running amok" echoed through Congress (CQ 1981). A political opportunity for sweeping policy changes emerged during this period because the ESA's authorization had lapsed. But since environmental issues were still high on the broader political agenda and support for the ESA remained generally strong in the legislative and executive branches, the policy changes receiving serious legislative attention called for increased flexibility through incremental modifications rather than a substantial statutory overhaul.

After some modest debate, Congress reauthorized the ESA in 1978 with few amendments (P.L. 95-632). The two most significant additions were an amendment requiring the secretary of the interior to consider economic impacts when designating critical habitat and another creating a seven-member review board, commonly referred to as the "God Squad," with the power to exempt federal projects and allow extinctions to occur in extraordinary cases. This committee convened for the first time in January 1979 to consider the Tellico Dam. In its historic first decision, the God Squad refused an exemption for Tellico (CQ 1981). Proponents of the dam, however, continued to push for completion during yet another round of ESA reauthorization bills in 1979. Following some legislative efforts that many policy leaders perceived as interdependent, the Tellico Dam was allowed to open, and the ESA was reauthorized for three more years without changes (P.L. 96-159).

IN THE WAKE OF TELLICO DAM

Only a few years after the Tellico Dam case, the ESA was again the subject of an intense judicial evaluation. The Sierra Club filed a lawsuit against the state of Hawaii alleging that the latter's use of public land for grazing was damaging the habitat of an endangered species—a bird known as the Palila. The plaintiffs alleged that destroying a listed species' habitat was a taking according to the FWS's regulations and the ESA's statutory language. The 1981 case (*Palila v. Hawaii*) focused primarily on whether the FWS's 1975 regulatory definition of harm (one of the actions considered a "taking" under the ESA), which included the unintentional destruction of a listed species habitat, was consistent with the statute. The judge in the case upheld the regulatory definition. His decision was based in part on the Supreme Court's 1978 Tellico Dam opinion, in which the Court noted the indisputable connection between habitat and species identified in the legislation (Percival et al. 1992). The ESA's legal power to protect land (that is, property) in addition to species was affirmed.

The FWS under the Reagan administration disagreed with the decision, arguing that the regulatory definition of harm was "inconsistent with the intent of Congress" and "exceeded the scope of authority conferred by section 9" (FWS 1981a). Although it encountered stiff opposition from environmental groups, the FWS rewrote its own regulations following the 1981 Palila case and defined harm as "direct, physical injury to an individual member of the wildlife species" (FWS 1981b). By doing so, the executive branch was able to make policy modifications that it thought would limit the ESA's scope to the direct protection of species—not their habitat—without actually changing the statute. The FWS under President Ronald Reagan also attempted to impede implementation by slowing the decision-making process for candidate species, essentially halting new additions to the endangered species list.

In the legislative branch, the act was under fire from congressional members, industry lobbyists, and some administration officials, all of whom were promoting an image of the ESA as too stringent. Many representatives from these groups felt that "more weight should be given to the expected economic values of a project or action as opposed to the potential values of the plant or animal that might be threatened by it" (Webster 1982, 11). A national mood swing toward fiscal conservatism, a focus on economic growth over environmental protection by the Reagan administration, and a lapse in the statute's authorization in 1982 all provided political opportunities for policy change. The act, however, had key support from some powerful committee chairs and environmental groups who pushed reform legislation designed to counteract the Reagan administration's efforts to block ESA implementation.

The act was reauthorized in 1982 with minimal debate and only incremental changes despite the potential for enormous controversy. Driven by concern that takings prohibitions could conflict with property uses, new provisions in the law allowed property owners to file for incidental take permits if the "taking" did not jeopardize the species' existence and if the landowner filed an acceptable habitat conservation plan. Proponents of the ESA successfully added modifications that they thought would improve implementation, including a one-year deadline for listing decisions and a mandate to base listing decisions solely on biological considerations (Shabecoff 1982b).

The remainder of the 1980s saw continued political and legal disputes regarding the ESA, including yet another example of judicial evaluation in 1986 involving the Palila case and the regulatory definition of harm. The same judge from the original Palila case ruled in a nearly identical lawsuit, referred to as Palila II, that the FWS's 1981 changes to the regulatory definition of harm were invalid because they failed to protect listed species' habitat. The ruling made it clear that species protection in the act was inextricably linked to habitat protection: "habitat destruction that prevents the recovery of the species by affecting the essential behavioral patterns causes actual injury to the species and effects a taking under section 9 of the Act" (quoted in Percival et al. 1992).

Some industry groups voiced concern over the Palila II decision and called for dramatic legislative changes in ESA's statutory language to avoid disputes over endangered species habitat on private and public property. However, Congress did not make significant changes in the act when the ESA was reauthorized in 1988 (P.L. 100-478). This five-year renewal marked the last time the ESA was reauthorized, as the 1990s witnessed a series of organized and powerful campaigns not only to change the act but to completely rescind it as well.

THE ESA IN THE 1990s

The act's new troubles began early in the 1990s, when it took center stage in a bitter dispute concerning the northern spotted owl and old-growth logging in the Pacific Northwest. This issue served as a focusing event for conflicts between species protection and economically oriented land uses such as logging (owls vs. jobs). As in the Tellico Dam case, regional controversy had been brewing over the appropriate balance between environmental protection and resource use for many years prior to the ESA's involvement. The ESA entered the debate in 1990, when the FWS listed the northern spotted owl as a threatened species and determined that more than 50% (roughly 4.2 million acres) of the owl's suitable habitat was on timber production land managed by federal agencies (Pytte 1990). Tensions heightened when the FWS identified 11.6 million acres in the region as critical habitat for the spotted owl (Davis 1991). Given the ESA's stringent provisions, some logging practices on public and private land within that area would have to be stopped, diminished, or altered.

An enormous political battle erupted pitting timber companies and local communities dependent on timber harvests against environmentalists concerned about the loss of old-growth forests (the owl's preferred habitat). Many in the latter group argued that timber companies were putting profits before both people and the environment by using more automated logging techniques, by removing trees too rapidly, and by destroying ancient ecosystems. Logging advocates warned that saving the owl throughout its range would cause massive economic losses, prompting calls for legislative reform. Detractors of the ESA began promoting a negative image of the act as an extremist law that made plants and animals a higher priority than people (Egan 1992; Schneider 1992). Sensing that a political window of opportunity was opening as reauthorization efforts began in 1992, members of Congress from the Northwest, officials from the Bush administration, and lobbyists representing a myriad of business interests led a coordinated attack on the ESA (CQ 1993a; Conservation Fund 1992). Even the secretary of the interior (the executive department that houses the FWS), Manuel Lujan, called for reform (Davis 1991). But the predicted political battle never materialized, as the ESA received little legislative attention in 1992, partially because the 102nd Congress was entangled in other environmental policy battles (such as reauthorization of the Clean Water Act) (Davis 1992b). As a result, ESA reauthorization lapsed.

In 1993 and 1994 (the 103rd Congress), a new element in the ESA debate emerged—private property rights. Property rights groups alleged that in some cases the ESA was imposing restrictions on the use of private property, resulting in economic losses so dramatic that the government was in effect seizing the land (CQ 1993b). Some property owners and their congressional advocates argued that such action constituted a "taking" but not the kind prohibited by the ESA (Rolston 1993). Instead, they alleged a taking forbidden by the Fifth Amendment of the Constitution, wherein the government is prohibited from taking private property for public use without just compensation.

With the ESA proponents still reeling from negative publicity concerning the spotted owl, a powerful property rights movement initiated legislative campaigns either to require compensation for ESA-related economic losses or to dismantle the 20-year-old statute (Stevens 1993a). Two policy images were being pitted against each other as the belief in property rights was being used to attack species protection efforts. Furthermore, some environmentalists were criticizing the ESA because it only protects individual species already on the verge of extinction and does nothing to prevent additional species or communities of species from becoming endangered (Doremus 1991; Spitzburg 1994). These sentiments were echoed by Secretary of the Interior Bruce Babbitt, who argued that it was time to shift away from single-species preservation and move toward "whole-ecosystem" conservation (Stevens 1993b).

Given the calls for changes to the act from numerous sides, some action on the ESA was expected in the 103rd Congress. In agenda-setting terms, both proponents and opponents drew attention to the act's problems, while reauthorization hearings provided ample political opportunities to make changes. However, no viable policy solutions emerged from all the reform rhetoric, partly because both sides seemed unwilling to work out a compromise and many congressional members were busy with other issues, such as an economic recession and an upcoming congressional election in which the Republicans were waging an aggressive campaign to garner a majority of seats in both the Senate and the House. At the conclusion of the 103rd Congress, the ESA remained unchanged and unauthorized.

Because of a well-organized and well-orchestrated campaign effort in 1994, the political climate changed in the 104th Congress. Republicans won control of both congressional chambers for the first time in decades. In the House, most of the incoming and returning Republican legislators had pledged to collectively and aggressively pursue the Republican Party's conservative agenda, titled the "Contract with America," which included comprehensive protection of property rights. ESA detractors portrayed the ESA as a prime example of oppressive federal regulations that hampered the economy and impinged on property rights. Democratic committee and subcommittee chairs who had been major obstacles in the past were replaced by Republicans, many of whom were openly hostile to the ESA.

The necessary policy conditions for dramatic modifications, according to both Kingdon (1995) and Baumgartner and Jones (1993), were beginning to materialize for the ESA. Not only were the political opportunities present (such as a landslide victory for Republicans and reauthorization hearings) and the attention paid to the ESA's alleged problems significant, but also the shift in party control had changed the political composition of Congress so dramatically that both chambers were essentially new venues.

Although very little legislative action associated with the ESA was taken in the Senate, the House was a different story.

The House Resources Committee assembled an Endangered Species Task Force charged with drafting reauthorization legislation. The task force held seven hearings throughout 1995 in regions reportedly hit hard by ESA restrictions, such as Washington, California, and Texas. Holding field hearings ensured that each meeting was filled with testimony from local landowners portraying an image of the ESA as a vehicle for property seizure. Based in part on these hearings, a bill was introduced designed to make habitat conservation on private property voluntary and required government compensation for ESA-related property devaluations greater than 20% (Beneson 1995; Cushman 1995). Both provisions would have strongly deterred federal efforts to protect listed species' habitat on private land. Despite strong prospects for passage, the Republican leadership tabled this legislation in part because the House was embroiled in a high-profile budget battle with the Clinton administration (CQ 1995). Republican leaders promised an ESA overhaul in the second session, but such efforts were soon abandoned in light of the public's largely negative reaction to the efforts of Republicans in the first session to roll back or revise the ESA and other popular environmental laws. The Republicans ceased almost all legislative activity in 1996 that could be construed as antienvironmental (Freedman 1996a), and the ESA once again emerged intact despite the grim forecast provided by many.

While the organized, persistent attacks common throughout the early to mid-1990s were not able to modify the ESA's statutory language, the act did undergo some dramatic changes in other policy areas, especially implementation practices. The most notable example was the FWS's unprecedented increase in the use of habitat conservation plans (HCPs), an ESA option for developing compromises between private land use and species protection that had been largely unused for almost a decade. The FWS had approved only five HCPs between 1982 and 1991. By September 1994, 36 HCPs were operational (Lehman 1995). Controversies surrounding property rights and species led to an even greater emphasis on HCPs as the FWS stepped up its own efforts to streamline the process (Lehman 1995) and approved roughly 60 new HCPs by September 1995, bringing the total number of plans up to 100 (FWS 2000).

The coordinated and aggressive attacks on the ESA that transpired primarily in the 103rd and 104th Congresses were replaced by persistent but much less intense debates over reauthorization since 1996. Staunch ESA opponents have consistently refused to consider any ESA renewal that does not dramatically weaken the act's legal ability to block federal and private development. On the other hand, biodiversity proponents have successfully deterred significant overhaul bills that they feel go too far and have repeatedly called for changes in the act that enhance implementation and/or habitat protection efforts (Carroll et al. 1996; Rohlf 1994). Meanwhile, Congress has annually appropriated funds for ESA implementation even though its authorization lapsed in 1993.

The ESA's history demonstrates that political attention does not always result in significant policy change. However, incremental changes are quite common when political windows open, as was the case for the ESA during the late 1970s and early 1980s. The unsuccessful efforts in the 1990s to substantially change or completely repeal the ESA failed partly because it often takes a highly unique set of political circumstances to overcome public support for a policy in addition to the bureaucracy and special interests that develop in response to policy. While the act was not significantly altered by the close scrutiny it received in the late 1980s and throughout the 1990s, the FWS did change its administration of the act (the use of HCPs) in response to demands from ESA supporters and detractors alike. Accordingly, we now turn to the FWS's overall implementation record.

The Politics of Implementation

Having considered the political context and history of the ESA, we now ask how this policy has fared in the hands of the executive branch. One way political scientists evaluate policy success is by looking at policy outputs—

actions taken by government to achieve policy goals (Lester and Stewart 1996). In the ESA's case, outputs would include listings, recovery plans, critical habitat designations, consultations, and expenditures.

The first list published pursuant to the 1973 legislation contained 109 endangered species. That list grew enormously in the following years. By 2000, it contained 706 domestic plants and 480 domestic animals (the list also has foreign species, which are not subject to many of the act's stipulations) (FWS 2000). Roughly 150 candidate species were waiting in line for full review under the act's listing procedures in 2000 (FWS 2000), a number significantly lower than the 3,700 candidates in 1992 (Chadwick 1995). The FWS was criticized in the early 1990s for this backlog of species in addition to a poor record on recovery plans and critical habitat designations.

Of those 1,186 currently listed species, 885, or 75%, have approved **recovery plans** (FWS 2000). This is a significant improvement from 1995, when only 54% of the 956 listed species had such plans, and 1992, when a little less than 50% had approved plans. Even lower than the percentage of species with recovery plans in the early 1990s was the number of species with **critical habitat designations**. In 1992, 16% (105 of 651 domestically listed species) had such designations. These figures were down to roughly 11% (124 of 1,082 species) in 1997 and 10% (120 of 1,186) in 1999. The lack of critical habitat designations may appear low, but considering the potential for enormous political conflict over land uses and economic losses on property containing critical habitat (factors the FWS is required by law to take into consideration), the number is not surprising.

The FWS has often claimed that implementation has been hampered over the years by resources insufficient to effectively perform the monumental tasks outlined in the statute. This problem is common to most of the laws under FWS jurisdiction, an agency that continues to be a bit player within the Department of the Interior and as such is perennially understaffed, underfunded, and underrepresented in the department's power structure (Tobin 1990). Funding for the act in constant dollars stayed relatively constant from 1974 until the 1990s (except for a slight dip during the

Reagan administration) despite enormous growth in the number of species listed. However, ESA funding has risen steadily over the past five years.

It is clear from its interagency consultation record that the FWS has consulted regularly with federal agencies concerning the ESA. The FWS has conducted more than 200,000 consultations from the act's passage to the mid-1990s. The FWS issued jeopardy opinions (in essence, a formal request for changes) in only 754 cases, or 0.3% (FWS 1997; Jantzen 1981). Although its record of cooperation with federal entities is impressive, the FWS only recently heightened its efforts to work with private landowners through HCPs. Between 1983 and mid-1994, only 36 HCPs were approved (Lehman 1995). By early 1997, the FWS had issued 212 permits (FWS 1997), a figure that climbed to 269 by early 2000 (FWS 2000). This rise in HCPs was partly an effort to mitigate the political controversy surrounding the ESA and property rights by demonstrating the FWS's willingness to balance development and species protection.

All the outputs reported here provide some indication of governmental effort, but they do not tell us whether those efforts are actually fixing the problem. Because money is being spent on outputs and, in many cases, money is being lost because of policy restrictions imposed on the public and private sectors, it is politically advantageous for bureaucrats and politicians to demonstrate a policy's effectiveness (that is, benefits), especially when the costs are high. For evidence of policy success, scientists attempt to measure outcomes—measures of change in the condition or problem that the policy was designed to address. Unfortunately, outcomes typically are much more difficult to measure than outputs, especially for biodiversity protection. We would need data that could tell us whether a species is recovering, its habitat is being maintained, and future threats are being mitigated. Such information is often expensive and subjective. The FWS claimed that 60% of listed species were stable or improving in 1994.

The delisting of listed species due to recovery would be another place to look for ESA success stories. However, only 29 species have been removed from the list over the years, 7 due to extinction and 12 due to recovery, while most of the remainder turned out not to be endangered after all

(50 CFR 424.11). The FWS points to the fact that less than 1% of listed species have gone extinct as evidence of policy success (FWS 2000).

The Future of U.S. Biodiversity Policy

A political battle still rages to determine whether the ESA has succeeded or failed and whether it must be strengthened or weakened. Attempts to reauthorize the statute will certainly spark debates over the "appropriate" balance between land use and species protection. Referring to them as the "quiet revolution" in conservation, the FWS touts HCPs as an effective tool for simultaneously protecting species and allowing economic growth (FWS 1998). However, these plans have been sharply criticized by some developers who say they are costly and time consuming, while some scientists and environmentalists charge that many of these plans are both inadequate in terms of species protection and inconsistent with the act's stated goals. In a recent assessment of the science used to develop hundreds of HCPs across the nation, a team of researchers representing several universities found that many were "scientifically inadequate" despite the ESA's statutory mandate to use "the best scientific data available" when drafting HCPs (National Center for Ecological Analysis and Synthesis 1997).

Others have been critical of HCPs and the ESA in general for focusing efforts on one particular species and its habitat rather than protecting whole ecosystems (Grumbine 1994; Yaffee 1996). The latter could provide a means by which to protect numerous populations of both healthy and imperiled species simultaneously in an effort to maintain ecosystem structure and function. Without this ability, the formal power of the ESA is limited only to rescuing species in the most dire straits (a task that has proven difficult) rather than taking a more preventive approach that would curtail the destruction of healthy species and habitat. The FWS adopted a document in 1994 titled the *Ecosystem Approach to Fish and Wildlife Conservation* and is currently developing an "ecosystem approach" that incorporates economic as well as ecological concerns into management decisions (FWS 2000). However, it is unlikely that an ecosystem strategy would be politically less challenging than the species by species one currently in place. Regardless of what form it takes, biodiversity protection cannot happen without habitat protection (National Research Council 1995), meaning that conflicts over property rights and economic development are unavoidable.

So what does the future hold for biodiversity policy in the United States? The answer to that question depends on a myriad of factors, including congressional and presidential elections, reauthorization of the ESA or the creation of new biodiversity policy, funding for ESA programs, continued loss of habitat, public opinion on environmental issues, and special interest campaigns both for and against biodiversity policy, to name just a few. If the past is prologue, then the political history of the ESA reveals that it takes an unusual set of political circumstances to create strong biodiversity policy. Once policy is enacted, the law will have to endure periods of intense social, legal, and political evaluation that may lead to changes. Moreover, implementing biodiversity policy is challenging because it often imposes economic losses and political expenditures that are easily measured in dollar values, while the benefits (that is, outcomes) are largely intangible, deferred to the future, and difficult to measure. Time, however, is not on the side of biodiversity. For now, we can optimistically expect to "hold the line" on extinctions, but real breakthroughs in protecting biodiversity (protecting ecosystems and preventing species from reaching endangered or threatened status) will require innovations in science, politics, and policy.

REFERENCES

Baumgartner, Frank R., and Bryan D. Jones. 1993. *Agendas and instability in American politics.* Chicago: University of Chicago Press.

Beneson, Bob. 1995. House panel votes to restrict Endangered Species Act. *Congressional Quarterly Weekly Report* 53, no. 40 (October 14):3136–37.

Bonine, John, and Thomas McGarity. 1984. *The law of environmental protection.* St. Paul, Minn.: West.

Carroll, R., C. Augspurer, A. Dobson, J. Franklin, G. Orians, W. Reid, R. Tracy, D. Wilcove, and J. Wilson. 1996. Strengthening the use of science in achieving the goals of the Endangered Species Act. *Ecological Applications* 6:1–11.

Chadwick, Douglas. 1995. Dead or alive: The Endangered Species Act. *National Geographic* 187, no. 3 (March 1995):2–42.

Congressional Quarterly. 1966. *Congressional Quarterly almanac.* Washington, D.C.: Congressional Quarterly, Inc.

———. 1972. *Congressional Quarterly almanac.* Washington, D.C.: Congressional Quarterly, Inc.

———. 1973. *Congressional Quarterly almanac.* Washington, D.C.: Congressional Quarterly, Inc.

———. 1981. *Congress and the nation volume V 1977–1980.* Washington, D.C.: Congressional Quarterly, Inc.

———. 1993a. *Congress and the nation volume VIII 1989–1992.* Washington, D.C.: Congressional Quarterly, Inc.

———. 1993b. *Congressional Quarterly almanac.* Washington, D.C.: Congressional Quarterly, Inc.

———. 1995. *Congressional Quarterly almanac.* Washington, D.C.: Congressional Quarterly, Inc.

Congressional Research Service. 1982. *A legislative history of the Endangered Species Act of 1973, as amended in 1976, 1977, 1978, 1979, and 1980.* Washington, D.C.: U.S. Government Printing Office.

Conservation Fund. 1992. The Endangered Species Act: Controversial listings sharpen reauthorization debate. *Land Letter* 11, no. 3 (January 20):3.

Cushman, John. 1995. House GOP leaders propose to ease Endangered Species Act. *New York Times,* September 8, A14(N), A20(L).

Davis, Philip. 1991. BLM calls on God Squad to let its timber go. *Congressional Quarterly Weekly Report* 49, no. 37 (September 14):2612.

———. 1992a. Critics say too few jobs, owls saved under God Squad plan. *Congressional Quarterly Weekly Report* 50, no. 20 (May 16):1334–35.

———. 1992b. Economy, politics threaten Species Act renewal. *Congressional Quarterly Weekly Report* 50, no. 1 (January 4):16–18.

Doremus, H. 1991. Patching the ark: Improving legal protection of biological diversity. *Ecology Law Quarterly* 18:265–333.

Downs, Anthony. 1972. Up and down with ecology: The issue attention cycle. *The Public Interest,* summer, 38–50.

Egan, Timothy. 1992. Strongest federal law may become endangered species. *New York Times,* May 26, A1.

———. 1995. Industry reshapes Endangered Species Act. *New York Times*, April 13, A9(N), A20(L).

Fischer, Hank. 1993. Testimony on behalf of Defenders of Wildlife, hearing titled *ESA Incentives to Encourage Conservation by Land Owners*, before the House Committee on Merchant Marine and Fisheries, Subcommittee on Environment and Natural Resources, 103rd Cong., 1st sess., October 13, 1993. Serial 103-65, 7–9.

Freedman, Allan. 1996a. A change in the environment. *Congressional Quarterly Weekly Report* 54, no. 9 (March 2):544.

———. 1996b. Republicans strive to gain environmental advantage. *Congressional Quarterly Weekly Report* 54, no. 20 (May 18):1384–86.

———. 1997. Hard-won coalition holds as species bill advances. *Congressional Quarterly Weekly Report* 55, no. 39 (October 4):2393–94.

Fish and Wildlife Service. 1981a. Endangered and threatened wildlife and plants; proposed redefinition of "harm." *Federal Register* 46:29490, 29492.

———. 1981b. Endangered and threatened wildlife and plants; final redefinition of "harm." *Federal Register* 46:54748.

———. 1982. Appendix to testimony of Robert Jantzen, director FWS, at a hearing before the Senate Subcommittee on Environmental Pollution, 97th Cong., 1st sess., December 8 and 10, 1981. Serial 97-H34.

———. 1997. Endangered species general statistics. www.fws.gov.

———. 1998. *Habitat conservation plans: The quiet revolution.* Available at www.fws.gov.

———. 2000. Endangered species home page. www.fws.gov.

Goodin, Robert E., and Hans-Dieter Klingemann. 1996. *A new handbook of political science.* New York: Oxford University Press.

Grumbine, R. Edward, ed. 1994. *Environmental policy and biodiversity.* Washington, D.C.: Island Press.

Jantzen, Robert. 1981. Testimony before the Senate, Subcommittee on Environmental Pollution, 97th Cong., 1st sess., December 8 and 10, 1981. Serial 97-H34.

Kingdon, John W. 1995. *Agendas, alternatives, and public policies.* New York: HarperCollins.

Lehman, William. 1995. Reconciling conflicts through habitat conservation planning. *Endangered Species Bulletin* 20, no. 1 (January–February):16–19.

Lester, James P., and Joseph Stewart. 1996. *Public policy: An evolutionary approach.* Los Angeles: West.

Mazmanian, Daniel A., and Paul A. Sabatier, 1989. *Implementation and public policy.* Lanham, Md.: University Press of America.

Menell, Peter S., and Richard B. Stewart. 1994. *Environmental law and policy.* Boston: Little, Brown.

National Center for Ecological Analysis and Synthesis. 1997. *Using science in habitat conservation plans.* Washington, D.C.: American Institute of Biological Sciences.

National Research Council. 1995. *Science and the ESA.* Washington, D.C.: National Academy Press.

Percival, Robert, Alan Miller, Christopher Schroeder, and James Peape. 1992. *Environmental regulation.* Boston: Little, Brown.

Plater, Zygmunt, Robert Abrams, and William Goldfarb. 1992. *Environmental law and policy: Nature, law and society.* St. Paul, Minn.: West.

Pytte, Alyson. 1990. Bush hedges on spotted owl, forces Congress to choose. *Congressional Quarterly Weekly Report* 48, no. 26 (June 30):2043–44.

Rohlf, D. 1994. Six biological reasons the Endangered Species Act doesn't work and what to do about it. In *Environmental policy and biodiversity.* Edited by R. E. Grumbine. Washington, D.C.: Island Press, 181–200.

Rolston, Holston, III. 1993. Life in jeopardy on private property. In *Balancing on the brink of extinction.* Edited by Kathryn Kohm. Washington, D.C.: Island Press.

Schneider, Keith. 1992. U.S. settles suit to save more threatened species. *New York Times,* December 16, A1(L).

Shabecoff, Philip. 1982a. House votes to add 3 years to endangered species law. *New York Times,* June 9, 6(N), A8(L).

———. 1982b. Views of 3 agencies conflict on endangered species law. *New York Times,* March 9, 9(N), A16(LC).

Shenon, Philip. 1990. Agency's flaws linked to extinction of endangered species. *New York Times,* October 18, A16 (N), A18(L).

Spitzburg, L. 1994. The reauthorization of the Endangered Species Act. *Temple Environmental Law and Technology Journal* 13:193–233.

Stevens, William. 1993a. Battle looms over U.S. policy on species. *New York Times,* November 16, B5(N), C1(L).

———. 1993b. Interior secretary is pushing a new way to save species. *New York Times,* February 17, A1.

Stone, Deborah. 1997. *Policy paradox: The art of political decision making.* New York: Norton.

Tobin, R. J. 1990. *The expendable future: U.S. politics and the protection of biological diversity.* Durham, N.C.: Duke University Press.

Vig, Norman, and Michael Kraft. 2000. *Environmental policy in the 1990s.* 4th ed. Washington, D.C.: Congressional Quarterly Press.

Webster, Bayard. 1982. Possible revisions in the Endangered Species Act. *New York Times*, March 1, 11(N), D10(LC).

Wilson, Edward O. 2002. *The future of life.* New York: Knopf.

Wilson, James, ed. 1980. The politics of regulation. In *The Politics of Regulation*, New York: Basic, 357–94.

Yaffee, Steven Lewis. 1982. *Prohibitive policy: Implementing the federal Endangered Species Act.* Cambridge, Mass.: MIT Press.

———. 1996. *Ecosystem management in the United States: An assessment of current experience.* Washington, D.C.: Island Press.

S U G G E S T E D   R E A D I N G S

Brick, Philip D., and R. McGreggor Cawley, eds. 1998. *A wolf in the garden: The land rights movement and the new environmental debate.* Lanham, Md.: Rowman & Littlefield.

Grumbine, R. Edward, ed. 1994. *Environmental policy and biodiversity.* Washington, D.C.: Island Press.

Kingdon, John W. 1995. *Agendas, alternatives, and public policies.* New York: HarperCollins.

Lester, James P., and Joseph Stewart. 1996. *Public policy: An evolutionary approach.* Los Angeles: West.

Mazmanian, Daniel A., and Paul A. Sabatier. 1989. *Implementation and public policy.* Lanham, Md.: University Press of America.

Menell, Peter S., and Richard B. Stewart. 1994. *Environmental law and policy.* Boston: Little, Brown.

Percival, Robert, Alan Miller, Christopher Schroeder, and James Peape. 1992. *Environmental regulation.* Boston: Little, Brown.

Rohlf, D. 1994. Six biological reasons the Endangered Species Act doesn't work and what to do about it. In *Environmental policy and biodiversity.* Edited by R. E. Grumbine. Washington, D.C.: Island Press, 181–200.

Tobin, R. J. 1990. *The expendable future: U.S. politics and the protection of biological diversity.* Durham, N.C.: Duke University Press.

Yaffee, Steven L. 1982. *Prohibitive policy: Implementing the federal Endangered Species Act.* Cambridge, Mass.: MIT Press.

———. 1994. *The wisdom of the spotted owl.* Washington, D.C.: Island Press.

———. 1996. *Ecosystem management in the United States: An assessment of current experience.* Washington, D.C.: Island Press.

The Global Challenge

Sharon L. Spray
and
Karen L. McGlothlin

Although scientists in this volume point out that assessing actual rates of global biodiversity loss is extremely difficult, there is little disagreement in the scientific community that current levels of habitat destruction are unprecedented in our current era of geological time and will have dramatic consequences for our modern world. Forest ecosystems that maintain an array of watershed functions, remove air pollutants, sequester carbon, moderate weather extremes, and provide food and medicinal goods are disappearing at alarming rates. Recent statistics indicate that total forest loss is at about 146,000 square kilometers (about 56,371 square miles) per year, with the loss of primary tropical forests, among the most ecologically diverse systems on earth, comprising more than 140,000 square kilometers

(54,054 square miles) of the yearly loss. Many of the world's remaining forests are fragmented as a result of development and consumption or damaged because of pollution and other deleterious environmental conditions and unable to support the diversity of life once associated with them (Bright 2003). Freshwater resources, under the pressure of a ballooning global population, will likely prove to be a critical problem as well. Freshwater systems provide crucially important drinking water for billions of people in the world and sustain freshwater ecosystems that cycle nutrients, provide aquatic habitat, filter pollution, and provide water transportation corridors and hydroelectricity. Once-abundant fish stocks, such as Atlantic cod and bluefin tuna, are now overfished to the brink of depletion, and many of the world's most aesthetically treasured and important animals from the top of the food chain, such as the tiger, black rhinoceros, jaguar, and red wolf, are near extinction. Although scientists in this volume concur that the rapid rates of biological diversity losses during our present geological era are attributable to human activity, causality remains a complex mix of direct and indirect sources that pose considerable challenges to policymakers around the world.

Included among the list of direct causes of biological diversity loss are the alteration of natural habitats through deforestation, mining, unsustainable levels of fishing and hunting, urbanization, and land conversion for agricultural purposes. Indirect causes include worldwide demand for energy, population growth, agricultural practices, acid rain, the introduction of nonnative species, and industrial pollution. New threats to biodiversity include the alteration of species diversity through biotechnology, desertification, and climate change. The bottom line is that we understand the severity of the problem and can even identify causes of the problem, but moving from science to policy is challenging at both the national and the international level.

Scientific evidence is often ignored in the development of policy for multiple reasons, including who controls power at the domestic level, a lack of public concern over the problem, the economic costs and benefits, and how those costs and benefits are distributed. Environmental policies compete for resources and public attention against the backdrop of other domestic pressures, such as education, the economy, social welfare, health care, and debt relief. This makes it extremely difficult to convince policy-makers and citizens that long-term investments in ecosystem mainte-nance, climate change mitigation strategies, changes in agricultural policy, and other policy approaches that are necessary to stabilize current trends in the loss of biodiversity should rank equally as high as investments in these other areas. For developing nations, air and water pollution, toxic waste, and the degradation of farmlands are far more pressing problems than endangered species loss, climate change, or ozone depletion. This is not to say that developing countries are unconcerned with global environ-mental problems such as the loss of biodiversity but that other immediate needs are of greater urgency.

Many developing countries are currently struggling to address rapidly increasing population rates that contribute to increasing levels of land conversion, resource extraction, and pollution. Demographers project that the world's population will grow from 6 billion to approximately 9 billion people by midcentury. But it is the combination of population growth with rapidly increasing consumption patterns that are contributing to alarming levels of biodiversity loss in many regions of the world.

Consumption has direct effects on the reduction of biodiversity through the overharvesting of plants and animals, mining, oil production, and land clearance for agriculture and urban growth. The level of biodi-versity may be indirectly affected as the result of pollution, depletion of soil nutrients, habitat destruction, and/or other forms of environmental disturbance that occur from the process of natural resource extraction:

> For example, fabricating automobiles and other metal-intensive products in Japan requires moving or processing a yearly capita equivalent of about 14 metric tons of ore and minerals. Growing the food required to feed a single U.S. resident causes about 15 metric tons of soil erosion annually. In Ger-many, producing the energy used in a year requires removing and replacing more than 29 metric tons of coal overburden for each German citizen quite

apart from the fuel itself or the pollution caused by its consumption. (Porter et al. 2000, 3)

For many years, consumption patterns have grown even more rapidly than population levels with most of the demand for consumer goods coming from the industrialized world (see table 7.1). In 1997, consumers in the world's most affluent countries (approximately 16% of the world's population) spent 80% of the money that funded private consumption. Of the total $18 trillion spent on private consumption, $14.5 trillion was spent by consumers in high-income countries (World Resources Institute 2001). Yet much of the environmental destruction and biodiversity losses associated with these high rates of consumption occurred in the developing world.

Many have argued that asking the world's poorest countries to implement policies to preserve their remaining intact ecosystems and to take additional environmentally conscious actions such as to reduce carbon dioxide emissions when industrialized countries have gotten rich exploiting

Table 7.1. A comparison of the consumption of selected resources and other consumables by consumers in developed countries and those in undeveloped countries. Statistics from Porter et al. (2000)

RESOURCE OR CONSUMABLE	CONSUMPTION BY PEOPLE IN THE TOP ONE-FIFTH OF AFFLUENT COUNTRIES	CONSUMPTION BY PEOPLE IN THE POOREST ONE-FIFTH OF COUNTRIES
Fish and meat	45%	5%
Total energy	58%	>1%
Paper	84%	1.10%
Vehicles	87%	>1%
Telephone lines	74%	1.50%

these very resources is hypocritical. Future efforts to address the loss of biodiversity on a global scale will require addressing current economic imbalances between resource consumers and producers, specifically, finding ways to link the environmental degradation costs associated with the production of goods to the benefits derived from such products.

The bottom line in the debate over the global loss of biodiversity is that no single country can stem the tide of current losses simply through domestic efforts. Yet it is extremely difficult, given diverse levels of national resources and issues of national sovereignty, to develop successful international agreements to address this environmental challenge.

International Cooperation on the Loss of Biological Diversity

The international communities' earliest efforts to preserve biodiversity came in the form of agreements to protect flora and fauna by concentrating on the prevention and spread of plant diseases, the development of seed banks, and the coordination of specific resource management goals. Many of these agreements remain viable and important in addressing this environmental challenge but remain highly deficient in mitigating overall declines in global biological diversity. An example of this approach is the **Ramsar Convention** negotiated in Ramsar, Iran, in 1971 (formally known as the Ramsar Convention on Wetlands of International Importance Especially as Waterfowl Habitat). Parties to this convention agree to preserve at least one wetlands site of "international importance" to maintain waterfowl habitat. Although it was a constructive step in international cooperation to address critical habitat loss associated with these important ecosystems, countries can honor their commitments to the treaty and still resist the development of domestic policy to reduce overall wetland losses (for example, the United States currently protects 17 wetlands sites totaling over a million hectares of protected wetlands under the Ramsar Convention, but it is estimated that wetlands in the United States are disappearing at an estimated rate of 58,500 acres annually (http://wetlands.fws.gov [accessed May 28, 2001]). As a result, this convention has been largely ineffective in mitigating the overall loss of wetland habitats worldwide.

The **Convention for the Protection of the World Cultural and Natural Heritage** is another international agreement meant to address the loss of biodiversity. This agreement, which has been signed by 150 countries, coordinates international financial, scientific, and technological support for sites of "outstanding physical, biological, and geological features; habitats of threatened plants or animal species and areas of value on scientific or aesthetic grounds or from the point of view of conservation" (www. unesco.org [accessed May 30, 2001]). Countries that sign this convention agree to designate at least one site of value to the entire global community as a natural or cultural heritage site and by doing so preserve valuable natural habitat that might otherwise be left unprotected from development or deterioration. Areas in the United States that are protected under this convention include Grand Canyon, Everglades, Redwood, and Yellowstone National Parks. This treaty, however, is extremely limited in scope and has had little effect on the rate of species loss on a global scale. In fact, the convention has had very limited success in assuring the protection of designated sites. Currently, Yellowstone National Park and Everglades National Park are listed as threatened under the convention's list of endangered sites of natural heritage, reinforcing the point that even with an international convention in place, protection is still a matter of domestic political will and resources.

The 1979 **Convention on the Conservation of Migratory Species of Wild Animals (CMS)**, also know as the **Bonn Convention**, is another important international convention designed to facilitate the preservation of endangered animals whose migratory patterns cross national boundaries and are dependent on more than one habitat for survival. Birds are good examples of the need for such an agreement (see Haskell, this volume). As an example, country A could be managing summer habitat for cranes quite well, while winter habitat in country B is being destroyed by urbanization or pesticide runoff. Therefore, the efforts of one country are useless in species protection without cooperation from the other. This treaty attempts to remedy this problem through a series of treaties between parties that are situated within the critical ranges of specified endangered animals.

The Bonn Convention, however, has two appendices that dictate different state responses. Appendix I includes a listing of species that are in danger of extinction. All parties to the treaty are obliged to protect animals on this listing. Appendix II lists species that are at high risk and in need of transboundary conservation efforts. In this case, CMS calls for the parties within the vital range of these threatened animals to form cooperative conservation agreements. Because there are domestic economic trade-offs and capital investments associated with conservation efforts, agreement on which species should be listed on appendix I or appendix II becomes highly political at both the domestic and the international level. Evidence for this can be found by looking at appendix I, which originally listed 40 species for international protection. Since that time period (some species actually have been delisted during this time period as well), appendix I has grown to a list of only 79 migratory species facing extinction—far less than the number of species that are presently in danger (see Gibbons and McGlothlin, this volume). The limited number of species that fall under the protection of this international agreement illustrates the limitations of negotiating species protection on a case-by-case basis.

The 1973 **Convention on International Trade in Endangered Species (CITES)** is far more comprehensive than the international agreements mentioned previously but has also had limited results. As the title suggests, CITES is a trade agreement rather than a conservation agreement. Chief among the criticisms of CITES as an agreement to reduce the loss of global biodiversity is that the convention, while it may restrict trade between signature parties, does not guarantee protective status or conservation programs within the states in which vulnerable populations reside. Nor does the convention promote conservation programs prior to listing. In other words, the convention is reactive rather than proactive in addressing biodiversity loss.

Parties to CITES agree to trade restrictions on flora and fauna based on assessments of species vulnerability. Parties use an elaborate series of trade permits and export and import controls to reduce trade in three categories of endangered species. The greatest level of international trade protection is given to species listed in appendix 1 of the treaty. Listings under this appendix are "all species threatened with extinction which are or may by affected by trade." Appendix 2 listings are those species whose populations are not currently threatened with extinction but may become threatened with extinction if trade is not strictly regulated. Appendix 3 listings are "subject to regulation within [a country's] jurisdiction for the purpose of prevention or restricting exploitation" of the species.

Yet legal and illegal trade in wildlife continues at an alarming pace. Michael Kraft (2001) indicates that "an estimated $20 billion a year in international trade in living and dead wildlife takes place, with perhaps $2–$3 billion of this in illegal trade" (176). The shortfall of CITES is complex. Many of the signature parties lack the financial resources to monitor compliance with the treaty and implement national strategies to protect vulnerable species. Critics also charge that the convention has too many loopholes. The convention actually allows party nations in some cases to disregard listings in the appendices. For example, on a showing of an overriding economic interest, party nations may within 90 days of a species listing make a "reservation: to appendix 1 or appendix 2 listings (appendix 3 reservations may be made at any time). To make a reservation means that a party does not accept the listing of a species in a particular appendix and therefore is not subject to the convention's trade prohibitions regarding that species (Switzer 2001). Parties may also ignore listings for reasons of scientific research and for specimens that were acquired prior to the convention. The result is that trade of vulnerable species does in some cases continue legally between parties to the convention.

It may not seem logical for the international community to allow loopholes that so clearly limit the effectiveness of an agreement, yet, as Phillipe Sands and Albert Bedecarre (1990) suggest, these exemptions were likely included to encourage greater state participation during the development stages of the agreement and were expected by the negotiating parties to be used infrequently. Clearly, the loopholes in the treaty have proven to be more problematic than likely anticipated, but once such loopholes have been built into a treaty, they are extremely difficult to reverse.

Loopholes that allow countries to avoid strict compliance with all aspects of international agreements are not uncommon. Concessions to important parties (those whose participation is critical to the effectiveness of the regime) are often unavoidable when trying to establish an agreement between multiple parties with different stakes in a final agreement. Gareth Porter, Janet Welsh Brown, and Pamela Chasek explain international cooperation as a "two-level game" in which negotiations take place between representatives of nation-states, while a second set of negotiations take place at the domestic level, where interest groups and other political influences must be satisfied to ensure acceptance of the agreement at the domestic level. This means that the positions taken by nation-states in international environmental negotiations reflect the domestic sociopolitical balances within each state (Porter et al. 2000). Treaties that attempt to address a wide range of problems and involve large numbers of parties have the greatest potential for exemptions and loopholes to accommodate the differing needs of states with vastly different internal pressures. Yet international cooperation on the loss of biodiversity is essential even if our past experience with other treaties indicates that it is extremely difficult to negotiate and implement effective international environmental agreements.

The most comprehensive international environmental treaty to address the loss of biological diversity is the **Convention on Biological Diversity (CBD)**, which entered into force in December 1993 and has since been signed by 175 countries and ratified by nearly all the original parties. This convention is the only international legal instrument that attempts to address the loss of biodiversity on a global scale through the promotion of strategies for ecosystem vitality rather than the protection of biological diversity on a case-by-case basis or within a particular ecosystem (such as wetlands, forests, or coastal zones).

The foundation of the CBD is an agreement among the parties that they will develop national strategies, plans, or programs to preserve biological diversity. Parties to the convention agree to pursue domestic strategies to ensure **sustainable development**—economic growth that takes place at a rate in which biodiversity can be preserved. The convention text states,

> The agreement covers all ecosystems, species, and genetic resources. It links traditional conservation efforts to the economic goal of using biological resources sustainably. It sets principles for the fair and equitable sharing of the benefits arising from the use of genetic resources, notably those destined for commercial use. It also covers the rapidly expanding field of biotechnology, addressing technology development and transfer, benefit-sharing and biosafety. Importantly, the Convention is legally binding; countries that join it are obliged to implement its provisions. (www.biodiv.org/doc/publications/guide.asp?id=action [accessed June 2, 2002)

The key wording of the agreement is that countries that sign the agreement are merely "obliged to implement" the agreement. International legal instruments (conventions and treaties) cannot be forcibly implemented. Nation-states remain sovereign with no higher world authority to force compliance. There are international environmental agreements that carry sanctions for noncompliance, such as the Montreal Protocol to eliminate chlorofluorocarbons, but the CBD is mostly a general statement of goals encouraging states to consider biodiversity conservation in the development and implementation of national policies. Article 3 of the CBD clarifies this by stating,

> States have, in accordance with the Charter of the United Nations and the principles of international law, the sovereign right to exploit their own resources pursuant to their own environmental policies and the responsibility to ensure that activities within their jurisdiction or control do not cause damage to the environment of other States or of areas beyond the limits of national jurisdiction. (www.biodiv.org/convention/articles.asp?lg=0&a=cbd-03 [accessed June 7, 2002)

Compliance is ultimately dependent on the political resolve and the resources available within each nation-state. Implementation of this treaty at the domestic level will require policy development and enforcement strategies for vastly different problems associated with the loss of biodiversity. For example, the policies to assess, restrict, and monitor the development, importation, and distribution of genetically modified organisms will be quite different from the policies needed to address deforestation, fragmentation, and degradation of forests.

Many countries simply do not have the institutional, organizational, or human capacity to develop national policies to comply with the treaty or even complete the biodiversity surveys required by the CBD to increase our global understanding of the problem. Without accurate data on current levels of biodiversity and trend information on use and declines in various resource categories, it will be extremely difficult for developed and developing nations to prioritize their conservation activities. There are financial mechanisms built into the CBD to assist developing countries in meeting their treaty obligations, but the details associated with the transfer of financial resources from developed to developing countries continue to be a point of contention, especially for the United States, which is one of the few countries that originally signed the CBD but never ratified the agreement.

As with the **Kyoto Protocol** (an international agreement to address global climate change), members of the U.S. Congress have expressed reluctance to ratify the treaty, fearing that the agreement could constrain economic growth. Senators from western states have lodged more specific objections stating that signing the CBD could obligate the United States to place limits on the use of domestic natural resources, such as grazing rights on public property or the confiscation of private land to develop habitat corridors. Members of Congress have also expressed concern over the level of financial obligation that the United States may incur in the future since the details of the treaty will be worked out in future meetings with the signature parties. Members of Congress have also raised questions about the convention's guidelines for intellectual property rights. As written, some members of Congress read the convention to suggest that American companies, particularly pharmaceutical companies, would have to share the benefits of products produced from genetic resources found elsewhere. Because most of the world's biodiversity exists in the tropical regions of developing countries and the markets and technology for developing those resources reside with the richer, industrialized nations, such as the United States, the guidelines could require domestic industries to share profits and patents with foreign countries, a condition that many members of Congress find nonnegotiable (*Congressional Record*, September 30, 1994).

Although the CBD far exceeds most nations' resolve to prioritize biodiversity conservation at this time, this international agreement is a positive step forward in developing international cooperation to address this global environmental challenge. This agreement will facilitate the establishment of international rules, guidelines, and norms of behavior to guide the stewardship of environmental resources, place the loss of biodiversity on national agendas, provide a framework for the sharing of important environmental and technical information between nations, and establish a series of meetings within the world community to continue efforts to address the loss of biodiversity at every level.

The real issue associated with stemming the present tide of biodiversity loss is one of political will and the extent to which human civilization will value biodiversity in the years to come. Authors in this volume point out that valuation of nature is complex. There is no globally accepted ethical framework to guide political and economic decision making associated with biodiversity preservation. Without such a common ethical valuation of nature, national and international policies will remain subject to the ebb and flow of political power and fluctuations of national and international economies. The solution to biodiversity loss, however, is not to retreat from global environmental conventions and treaties but rather to continue to strengthen these agreements while also working to address the pressures placed on biodiversity from population growth and patterns of unsustainable consumption.

REFERENCES

Bright, C. 2003. A history of our future. In *State of the world 2003: A Worldwatch Institute report on progress toward a sustainable society.* Edited by L. Starke. New York: Norton.

Kraft, Michael. 2001. *Environmental policy and politics.* New York: Longman.

Porter, Gareth, Janet Welsh Brown, and Pamela Chasek. 2000. Global environmental politics. Boulder, Colo.: Westview.

Sands, Phillipe J., and Albert P. Bedecarre. 1990. Convention of International Trade in Endangered Species: The role of public interest. *Boston College Environmental Affairs Law Review* 17(4):799–822.

Switzer, Jacqueline. 2001. *Environmental politics: Domestic and global dimensions.* 3rd ed. New York: St. Martin's.

World Resources Institute. 2001. *World resources 2000–2001: People and ecosystems: The fraying web of life.* Washington, D.C.: World Resources Institute.

Glossary

Abiotic—nonliving; the physical and chemical components of an environment that result in particular distributions and abundances of organisms.

Accretion—the addition of crust to a continent.

Agrichemicals—synthetically produced chemicals (such as fertilizers and pesticides) used in agriculture.

Alleles—alternative forms of genes.

Amphibians—the vertebrate class of animals that includes frogs, toads, salamanders, and caecilians.

Animal rights—these arguments claim that certain classes of animals—usually higher mammals—possess or should be accorded moral and/or legal rights that constrain our treatment of them. The philosopher Tom Regan has developed the most systematic rights-for-animals position in the literature of environmental ethics.

Animal welfare/liberation—these terms refer primarily to the philosopher Peter Singer's utilitarian approach to the ethical consideration of animals, a project that is centered on the moral significance of states of pleasure and pain, or "sentience." According to Singer, since many animals can experience pain, we must consider their interests when the consequences of our actions affect them. As a result, the political task is to free or "liberate" animals from any harmful treatment that we inflict on them.

Anthropocentrism—literally defined as "human centeredness," this term describes the worldview whereby nonhuman nature is viewed primarily in terms of its connections and contributions to human desires, values, and purposes; an approach to environmental ethics in which value is assigned to nature on the basis of what nature can do for humans (such as provide resources, recreation, and clean water).

Ash—fragments of material ejected into the air during a volcanic eruption.

Assurance colonies—live collections of seriously threatened or endangered animal or plant species that are kept in breeding colonies to provide options for the recovery of wild populations through reintroductions in the future.

Background extinction—a continuous, low-level rate of extinction that has occurred throughout the history of life.

Benthic—term that is used to refer to organisms that inhabit the bottom in an aquatic ecosystem.

Bequest value—a value that is derived from knowing that others will be able to benefit from a resource.

Binomium—the two-part "scientific name" given to a living organism, consisting of the generic and specific name.

Biocentric individualism—a nonanthropocentric approach in environmental ethics, commonly attributed to the philosopher Paul Taylor, that emphasizes the direct moral consideration of individual organisms (such as plants, trees, and animals) as opposed to biophysical "wholes," such as ecosystems or biotic communities.

Biocentrism—an approach to environmental ethics in which nature is viewed as having intrinsic value independent of what nature can do for humans.

Biodiversity—the cumulative variety of species, various genetic forms of species, and all other taxonomic levels that characterize an ecosystem; most often expressed as the number of living species present in a prescribed area or region.

Biodiversity hot spots—twenty-five global geographic regions that have been identified as areas in which the numbers of rare and endemic species is particularly high.

Biodiversity inventory—a process undertaken in order to record the kinds of plants or animals in selected taxonomic groups that are present in a prescribed area.

Bioindicators—organisms used to assess the health of ecosystems.

Biological control—the control of pest organisms by the introduction of organisms or their products.

Biological diversity—*see* Biodiversity.

Biotic—living; those living components of the environment that result in particular distributions and abundances of organisms (such as competition for food, space, and mates).

Bonn Convention—*see* Convention on the Conservation of Migratory Species of Wild Animals (CMS).

Bottleneck—a marked decrease in the size of a population that results in a decrease in genetic variability and leads to genetic homogeneity within the population.

Bottom trawling—a fishing method in which a ground chain, wooden boards, and a trawl net are dragged along the seabed, resulting in a disturbance of the organisms on the seafloor that causes them to enter the trawl net.

Breeding Bird Survey—annual survey of breeding birds in North America.

Brood—group of nestling birds in a nest.

Burgess Shale—fossil locality in British Columbia of Middle Cambrian period (about 520 million years ago) in which unusual, soft-bodied animals are preserved.

Bycatch—a term commonly seen in fishing literature that refers to nontarget species that are collected during trawling and discarded back into the water, in many cases injured, dead, or dying.

Cambrian period—period of time 543 to 490 million years ago in which most major groups of animals first appear in the fossil record.

Climate proxy—a data set that provides a historic (or prehistoric) record of climate, such as tree rings, oxygen isotopes, coral growth bands, and thicknesses of annual ice layers.

Community—the assemblage of different species of organisms living together and interacting in a defined geographic area or physical habitat.

Conservation biology—the scientific study of the factors that affect the maintenance, loss, and restoration of the plant and animal species that contribute to biological diversity.

Contingent valuation—valuation determined on the basis of answers to a series of hypothetical questions.

Convention for the Protection of World Cultural and Natural Heritage—an international agreement in which parties agree to designate at least one site of global value as a natural or cultural heritage site in order to preserve valuable natural habitat that might otherwise receive protection; this treaty went into effect in 1972.

Convention on Biological Diversity (CBD)—an international treaty signed into force in 1993; the only international treaty enacted to address the global loss of biological diversity through the promotion of ecosystem vitality.

Convention on the Conservation of Migratory Species of Wild Animals (CMS)—an international treaty designed to facilitate the preservation of endangered migratory animals that cross national boundaries and are dependent on more than one habitat for survival; this treaty went into effect in 1971.

Convention on International Trade in Endangered Species (CITES)—an international agreement between governments enacted to ensure that international trade in specimens of wild animals and plants does not threaten their survival; this treaty went into effect in 1973.

Cost-benefit analysis—a comparison of the costs and benefits of a proposed action.

Cretaceous/Tertiary (K/T) boundary—rock layer denoting the distinction between the Cretaceous and Tertiary periods in geologic history.

Cretaceous period—period of time between 144 million years ago and 65 million years ago in which the first fossils of many insect groups and the first flowering plants are found.

Critical habitat designation—the geographic area that includes the biological or physical features essential to the conservation of the species; federal actions that adversely modify critical habitat are prohibited under Section 7, but such designations have no regulatory impact on private land.

Cuckoldry—mating of a female with a male who is not her social partner.

Demand curve—a graphical illustration of the relationship between price and the quantity demanded of a good or service within a given period.

Demographic—relating to the study of the births, deaths, and age distribution of a population.

Deoxyribonucleic acid (DNA)—the double-stranded nucleic acid that forms the genetic material of all cells, some cellular organelles, and many viruses.

Direct valuation—valuation in terms of monetary units (such as dollars).

Ecocentrism—a nonanthropocentric approach, associated with environmental philosophers Holmes Rolston, III and J. Baird Callicott, among others, that emphasizes the direct moral consideration of ecological wholes (species, ecosystems, bioregions, and often the biosphere itself) rather than individual organisms; philosophers such as Rolston and Callicott argue that such collectives possess or should be accorded intrinsic value rather than simply instrumental, or use, value.

Ecological niche—the total of all the abiotic and biotic factors that affect how an organism interacts with other organisms in its environment.

Ecological research—the scientific study of the relationships of organisms to their physical, chemical, and biological environment.

Ecological reserve—a designated area in which organisms are protected from human-caused environmental degradation, species removal, and other unnatural dangers.

Ecology—the scientific study of the relationships of organisms to their physical and biological environment that seeks to understand the factors that determine the distribution and abundance of organisms within that environment.

Economics—the study of the allocation of scarce resources among competing ends.

Ecosystem—the combination of living (biotic) and nonliving (abiotic) systems in a defined area.

Ecosystem services—the conditions and processes through which natural ecosystems and the species that constitute them sustain and fulfill human life.

Edge habitat—an area at the intersection of two distinct habitats.

Efficiency—a condition under which no one can be made better off without making someone else worse off.

Element—a substance that consists of only one type of atom.

Enabling statute—the law passed by the U.S. Congress and signed by the president that empowers a particular executive agency to take action on a particular issue.

Endangered Species Act (ESA)—legislation passed in 1973 that protects plants and animals that are listed by the federal government as "threatened" or "endangered."

Endemic species—a species of living organism that is confined to a particular geographic region.

Endothermic—the regulation of body temperature by the internal production of heat (such as birds and mammals).

Environmental ethics—the branch of applied philosophy devoted to the exploration and defense of moral regard for nonhuman nature, emphasizing the status and content of environmental values and their claims on human attitudes and behaviors.

Equilibrium—the point of balance in the market for a good or service at which the quantity consumers demand equals the quantity producers supply.

Eukaryotic—possessing cells that have a distinct, double membrane-bound nucleus; other membrane-bound organelles including mitochondria, ribosomes and Golgi bodies, and linear deoxyribonucleic acid (DNA).

Executive branch—the government body charged with implementing and enforcing the law, including the president, cabinet members, governors, agency staff, and departmental staff.

Existence value—value derived from knowing that a resource exists, unrelated to present or future use of the resource.

Externality—a positive or negative effect felt beyond those causing the effect.

Extinction—the termination of species.

Fauna—the animals of a region.

Food web—a complex representation of all the feeding interactions of an ecological community.

Free rider—one who attempts to benefit from a good or service without paying for it.

Gene flow—the spread of alleles between local populations as a result of the migration of individuals between those populations.

Gene pool—the total of all the alleles of all the genes present in an interbreeding population.

Genes—a segment of deoxyribonucleic acid (DNA) that functions as the basic unit of heredity and is composed of a sequence of nucleotide bases that code for the production of protein or ribonucleic acid (RNA) products.

Global climate change—observed and predicted alteration in climate caused by human modifications of the atmosphere.

Greenhouse gases—atmospheric gases that cause the greenhouse effect. Examples include carbon dioxide (CO_2), methane (CH_4), ozone (O_3), and water vapor (H_2O).

Habitat fragmentation—the partitioning of large, continuous areas of habitat into smaller areas through the development of roads, dwellings, agricultural fields, and land-transforming activities.

Hedonic pricing approach—the evaluation of prices as determined by differences in quality or circumstances.

Imperfect competition—a condition of market power that permits sellers to charge prices above their incremental costs, restrict the quantities produced, or produce goods of inferior quality.

Imperfect information—a lack of information about factors relevant to the market for a good, including the available products and suppliers, prices, and the quality of goods.

Implementation—steps taken by government to carry out the objectives and actions set forth in a particular statute.

Indirect valuation—valuation in terms of nonmonetary units; measurements might be in terms of productivity, health levels, environment resources, or man-made resources.

Industrial Revolution—radical social and economic changes that occurred in the late 18th century as a result of the mechanization of production systems that shifted small-scale, home manufacturing to large-scale, factory production.

Instrumental value—the value an object or entity has by virtue of its contribution to the satisfaction of some specified goal, preference, or experience; in the environmental context, parts of nonhuman nature may be said to have instrumental value for humans if they are capable of being used in a direct, material sense (such as using a forest for timber) or in an indirect, nonmaterial sense (such as using a forest for passive recreation activities, such as hiking and bird-watching).

Interior habitat—habitat away from edges.

Internalization—when all the effects of a decision are felt by the decision maker.

Intrinsic value—the value an object or entity possesses apart from its instrumental value, which may be ascribed by a valuing agent or posited to objectively exist in the qualities of the object in question; another way of stating this is to observe that the object or entity is "valued for itself" or that it possesses "value in itself" regardless of any use that humans may put it to.

Invertebrates—multicellular animals without a backbone (spinal column).

Island biogeography—the study of the spatial distribution and abundance of animals or plants in relationship to the size and other characteristics of islands.

Isotope—one of two or more forms of an element. Isotopes of the same element have different numbers of neutrons in the nucleus but the same number of protons and electrons. Carbon has three isotopes: ^{12}C, ^{13}C, and ^{14}C.

Judicial branch—the government body responsible for judging the law, settling legal disputes, and punishing those who violate the law.

Keystone species—a species that has a disproportionately large impact on the ecosystem in which it is found, determining the species composition and function of that ecosystem.

Kill curve—summarizes the history of species extinctions over the past 600 million years for marine organisms. The curve is used to find the average time interval between extinction events of a given magnitude.

Kyoto Protocol—an international treaty signed in Kyoto, Japan, in 1997 that would commit the developed countries of the world to reduce carbon dioxide emissions and other greenhouse gases.

Legislative branch—the government body empowered to create laws and allocate funding for implementing those laws, including Congress, state legislatures, city councils, and so on.

Long-distance migrant—a bird whose winter distribution is separated from its summer distribution by a long distance, usually several hundred or thousand kilometers.

Mass extinction—an extinction event that affects greater than 50% of the species living at that particular time.

Megafauna—large animals, such as elephants and rhinoceros.

Microclimate—climate variation that occurs on a small scale and may be the result of a variety of factors, including elevation, aspect, and soil characteristics.

Milankovich cycles—periodic changes in the shape of the earth's orbit about the sun and the orientation of the earth's equator relative to the plane of the orbit.

Monitoring—the process of continual measurement of particular features during an ecological study.

Monoculture—a type of farming in which only a single crop species is cultivated.

Moral pluralists—those who recognize that our moral commitments may issue from a number of different, perhaps even incompatible, philosophical grounds, or "first principles"; in the case of the environment, this means that we should not expect there to be only one morally "right" way to relate to nature, one way of properly valuing the natural world, or one type of obligation to the environment; pluralists thus differ from *moral monists*, who do seek a single moral theory to guide all human–nature relationships.

Morphological—referring to the anatomical features of a plant or animal, including size and shape.

Natural variability—changes that occur within organisms or ecosystems that are unaffected by forces other than those normally and characteristically found in nature.

Nonanthropocentrism—the antithesis of anthropocentrism, this term describes a nonhuman-centered worldview (such as biocentrism or ecocentrism) whereby natural elements or processes are viewed from a perspective that does not appraise them on the basis of their contribution to human experience, values, or desires; rather, they are respected and appreciated as having some sort of intrinsic, or noninstrumental, value.

Nonmigratory—a bird that does not migrate.

Option value—value associated with the option to use a resource in the future.

Ordovician period—period of time beginning approximately 510 million years ago and ending approximately 445 million years ago that is well known for the diversity of marine invertebrates in the fossil record.

Overkill hypothesis—a hypothesis that states that the Pleistocene extinctions of many large mammals and birds are the result of human hunting.

Oversight hearings—congressional hearings focused on evaluating an executive agency's implementation of a law.

Paleozoic era—543 to 248 million years ago.

Passive-use value—value not associated with the hands-on use of a resource.

Pelagic—a term that is used to refer to organisms that inhabit the water column in an aquatic ecosystem.

Pleistocene—on the geologic time scale, the first epoch of time in the Quaternary period, from 1.8 million years ago to 10, 000 years ago; also referred to as the Ice Age.

Policy—a process or a series or pattern of government activities or decisions that are designed to remedy some public problem, either real or imagined.

Policy enactment—the process of transforming a bill proposed in Congress into a law; requires passage in both the House and the Senate in addition to the president's signature.

Politics—the constrained use of social power; the struggle for authoritative use of power or who gets what, when, and why.

Prokaryotic—possessing a cell that has no distinct nucleus, no membrane-bound cellular organelles, and no circular deoxyribonucleic acid (DNA).

Protistans—organisms belonging to the kingdom Protista, which includes a diverse array of eukaryotic organisms, primarily single-celled organisms, such as *Paramecium.*

Public good—a good whose mere existence makes it available to all and whose consumption by one person does not affect the consumption of others, such as national defense and radio broadcasts.

Punctuated equilibrium—the idea, conceived by Stephen Jay Gould and Niles Eldredge, that species evolve rapidly, perhaps in a few thousand years, and remain the same for the rest of their existence.

Radiometric dating—a method for measuring the age of objects using the decay rate of radioactive elements; different radioactive elements are used, depending on the possible age of the object, to minimize the error of the analysis.

Ramsar Convention—an international treaty originally negotiated in 1971 in Ramsar, Iran, in order to protect international wetland habitat for the purpose of maintaining waterfowl habitat.

Recovery plans—documents that detail the specific tasks needed to recover a listed species; they provide a blueprint for private, federal, and state cooperation in the conservation of threatened and endangered species.

Regression analysis—a statistical method of determining the effect of one or more variables on another variable, such as the effects of pollution levels, water, and sunlight on tree growth.

Reproductive success/output—the number of offspring produced by breeding organisms.

Resource extraction—the removal of natural resources, such as wood, ore, or water.

Rival good—a good whose consumption by one person affects its consumption by other people, such as food and clothing but not national defense.

Sedimentary rock—rock formed from materials transported and deposited by water, wind, and ice.

Selective breeding—the deliberate selection of individuals for breeding on the basis of desirable traits.

Short-distance migrant—a bird whose winter distribution and summer distribution overlap somewhat or are separated by a short distance.

Sink populations—populations that rely on dispersal from other areas to maintain themselves.

Source populations—populations that produce many dispersing offspring that can colonize other habitats.

Speciation—the process in which new species are formed.

Species—the largest unit or population of organisms that is capable of breeding successfully to produce viable offspring.

Species abundance—the number of individuals of a species in a specified area or population.

Species–area relationship—a mathematical relationship between the area of habitat and the number of species supported by that habitat; the larger the area of a particular habitat, the greater the number of species it can support.

Species distribution—the geographic area where members of a species live and reproduce.

Species evenness—a measure of biodiversity based on the proportional abundance of individuals of each species present in a prescribed area.

Species inventory—a list of the species of organisms occupying a particular geographic area or physical habitat.

Species richness—a measure of biodiversity based on the number of species of a selected taxonomic group that is present in a prescribed area.

Supply curve—a graphical illustration of the relationship between price and the quantity supplied of a good or service within a given period.

Sustainable development—development that strives to provide economic, political, and social progress with minimal environmental compromise and without unsustainable resource depletion.

Sympathy value—value derived from knowing that a species has survived; not associated with the ability to come into contact with the species.

Taxonomic group—an assemblage of organisms (such as all species in a genus or all amphibians) that are considered to be more closely related evolutionarily to other members of the assemblage than to other organisms.

Tectonics—plate tectonic activity; plate tectonics is the theory that the outer skin of the earth is divided into rigid plates that move and interact along their edges.

Trophic—pertaining to a specific type of nutrition.

Tsunami—a large wave train usually created by underwater earthquakes, explosive volcanism, and submarine landslides.

Tuff—a hardened ash.

Use value—value derived from the actual use of resources and their by-products.

Utilitarianism—term describing the moral theory that directs an individual, when given a choice of acting in a number of different ways, to choose that alternative that produces the best balance of benefits to harms for all individuals affected by the proposed action; while utilitarian justifications have often been attributed to destructive environmental behaviors (since exploiting nature's resources to benefit many people would be acceptable, provided that the correct calculation of benefits and harms over time was performed), it also has been extended by philosophers such as Peter Singer to take into account the benefits and harms our actions might have for nonhuman nature, especially sentient animals that can experience states of pleasure and pain.

Voice vote—a vote during which the individual participant's vote goes unrecorded.

Weak anthropocentrism/pragmatism—a worldview through which nature is seen as contributing to human experience, values, and desires but not in a consumptive or consumer-driven fashion; for the weak anthropocentrist, nature provides the context for a number of valued cultural experiences, including aesthetic enjoyment, recreation, education, and spiritual fulfillment; while nature here is valued for its contribution to human life, it is not reduced to a mere commodity to be exploited in the market.

Wildlife refuge—an area of specific habitat that is established in order to maintain species and ecosystems that are sheltered from human disturbance and development.

Willingness to accept—the smallest amount of money one would willingly accept to forgo a resource.

Willingness to pay—the largest amount of money one would be willing to pay in exchange for a resource.

Zoocentrism—the set of theoretical approaches in environmental ethics (led by philosophers such as Peter Singer and Tom Regan) that focus on the direct moral considerability and/or rights of nonhuman animals.

Index

Alvarez, Walter, 9, 11
amphibian populations, 47
animal welfare, 84–85, 88–89
anthropocentrism: concept of, 80–81; and nonanthropocentrism, 67–69, 84–87, 90–92; strong versus weak, 81–84
Arrowhead Mountain Lake Association, 76, 93

Babbitt, Bruce, 135
Bavarian pine vole, 44
BBS. *See* Breeding Bird Survey
biocentrism: versus anthropocentrism, 68–69; concept of, 85–86
biodiversity: definition of, xvi, 29–30; extinction effects on, 14; future of, 22–23; historical data on, 46–48; hot spots for, 37, *38*; human impact on, 3–4, 21–23, 33, 37, 39–43; importance of, 30–31; measurement of, 45–48; private versus public ownership and, 36; problems with concept of, 77; study of, 31–32, 49; threats to, 150; through time, 13. *See also* extinction of species
bioindicators, 56–57
biological integrity, 77
Bonn Convention (1979), 154–55
bottom trawling, xvii
Breeding Bird Survey (BBS), 59–60
Bush, George H. W., 134
Bush, George W., xv
bycatch, xvii

Callicott, J. Baird, 86–87, 91, 93
Carson, Rachel, 41
Carter, Jimmy, 112
case study approach, 55
catastrophism, 23
CBD. *See* Convention on Biological Diversity
charismatic megafauna, 32, 114
CITES. *See* Convention on International Trade in Endangered Species
classification of organisms, 12–13, 48
climate change. *See* global climate change
Clinton, Bill, 137
coal, 8
Coase, Ronald, 112
Cody, Martin L., 48
coffee plantations, and migrant birds, 66–67
Committee on Rare and Endangered Wildlife, 127
computers, personal, 13
Congress, U.S.: and Convention on Biological Diversity, 159–60; and Endangered Species Act, 129–38
conservation biology: bioindicators in, 56–57; issues in, 58
conservation, competing interests and, xviii–xix
Conservation International, 37
consumption, effects on biodiversity of, 151–52
continents, change in, 6
contingency, evolution and, 17–18

Contract with America, 136–37
Convention for the Protection of the World Cultural and Natural Heritage, 154
Convention on Biological Diversity (1993, CBD), 157–60
Convention on International Trade in Endangered Species (1973, CITES), 32, 155–57
Convention on the Conservation of Migratory Species of Wild Animals (1979, CMS), 154–55
convergence hypothesis, 90–94
cost-benefit analysis, 100–108, 113–16, 123–24
cowbirds, 64
Cuvier, Georges, 9, 23

Darwin, Charles, 15–18, 23
Department of the Interior, 127–28
developing countries, 151–53
Dewey, John, 83
dilemmas: coffee plantations and migrant birds, 66–67; habitat type and bird populations, 61–62; mute swans, 75–78, 93–94; northern spotted owl and logging, 133–34; wilderness areas, 69. *See also* environmental ethics
dinosaurs, 3–4, 9, 11, 15, 17
disease, 41

earth: study of (*see* geoscience); time factors in changes to, 7–8
eastern oysters, 33
ecocentrism, 86–87, 91
ecological reserves. *See* reserves, ecological
economics: consumer choice, 66–67, 70–71; consumption patterns, 151–52; cost-benefit analysis, 100–108, 113–16, 123–24; definition of, 99; market factors,

108–13; trade in vulnerable species, 155–57
ecosystems: and biodiversity, 36–37; definition of, 30; as focus of conservation, 135, 141, 157; as ultimate source of value, 86–87
Ehrenfield, David, 84
endangered species: factors contributing to, xvi; gene variability and, xviii. *See also* biodiversity; extinction of species
Endangered Species Act (1973, ESA), 32; background on creation of, 127–29; explanation of, 125–27; future of, 140–41; grizzly bears and, xiv–xv; implementation of, 138–40; in 1980s, 131–33; in 1990s, 133–38; reauthorization of, 131–35; and resource extraction, 70; and valuation of species, 114
Endangered Species Conservation Act (1969), 128
Endangered Species Preservation Act (1966), 127–28
Endangered Species Task Force (1995), 136
endemic species, 37
environmental ethics: background on, 78–81; debates within, 87–94; and songbird conservation, 67–69; theoretical principles of, 81–87. *See also* dilemmas
Environmental Ethics (journal), 86
ESA. *See* Endangered Species Act
ethics. *See* dilemmas; environmental ethics
Everglades National Park, 154
evolution, theory of, 15–18
exotic species, 40–41, 76–77
extinction of species: climate change and, 23–25; current figures on, 21–23; evolution and, 16–17; fossils as record of, 9; geographical

isolation and, 34–35; mass, 3–4, 7, 19; past-present comparisons of, 15, 22–23; process of, 18–20; public awareness of, 32; rate of, xvi, 44; Red List and, 43–45; theories of, 14–21

faunas, evolutionary, 13–14
Federal Trade Commission (FTC), 111
Fifth Amendment, of U.S. Constitution, 135
Fish and Wildlife Service, U.S.: and ecosystem approach, 141; and grizzly bears, xiv–xv; and habitat conservation plans, 137; and implementation of ESA, 138–40; and northern spotted owl, 134; and Palila bird, 131; and regulations concerning endangered species, 126, 131–32, 133
fish, species depeletion of, xvii
forests, xvii, 149–50; fossils, 8–9, 13–14
freshwater resources, 150
FWS. *See* Fish and Wildlife Service, U.S.

gene pools, xviii, 31
geoscience, 4–8
global climate change: and biodiversity, 42–43; and extinction, 4, 23–25; factors in, 7–8; through time, 5–6
God Squad (Endangered Species Act review board), 131
Gould, Stephen J., 17
gradualism, 23
Great Smoky Mountains All Taxa Biodiversity Inventory (GSM ATBI), 46
greenhouse effect. *See* global climate change
grizzly bears, debate over preservation of, xiii–xv

habitat conservation plans, 127, 137, 139, 140–41
habitat fragmentation, 35, 62–64
habitats: changes in songbird, 61–67; destruction rates of, 149; human impact on, 40; legal protection of, 126, 131–32, 133, 136–37
Hargrove, Eugene, 83–84
Hawaii, 131
heath hen, 20–21
humans: adaptation of environment by, 18; biodiversity impact of, 3–4, 21–23, 33, 37, 39–43; extinctions caused by, 24–25; population growth of, 39, 151. *See also* anthropocentrism
hunting: of black rhinoceri, 33; as extinction cause, 24–25. *See also* overharvesting

International Biodiversity Observation Year (2001), 32
international cooperation, 153–60
International Union for Conservation of Nature and Natural Resources (IUCN). *See* World Conservation Union
island biogeography, 34–36
IUCN. *See* Red List of Threatened Species; World Conservation Union

James, William, 83
Janzen, Dan, 46
Johnson, Lyndon, 128

Kempthorne, Dirk, xv
kill curve, 19, *20*
Kyoto Protocol, 159

labeling. *See* product information
"last man" example, 79–80
legislation, 32, 70, 121–23. *See also* *specific acts*

Leopold, Aldo, 79, 87
Lord Howe Island stick insect, 44
luck, evolution and, 17–18
Lujan, Manuel, 134

mangrove forests, xvii
Man's Responsibility for Nature
(Passmore), 80
Martin, Paul, 24
Milankovich cycles, 5–6
Montreal Protocol, 158
mute swans, 75–77, 93–94
Myers, N., 22

National Institute for Biodiversity
(INBio, Costa Rica), 46
nature: inherent worth of, 86;
instrumental value of, 81–82;
transformative value of, 82–83
Nature Conservancy, 114
Nixon, Richard, 128–29
Noah's Ark model, 103–4, 113–14
Norse, Elliott, 30
northern spotted owl, 133–34
Norton, Bryan, 82–83, 90–93
Norton, Gail, xv

organisms, classification of, 12–13, 48
overharvesting: of Asian turtles, 42; of
eastern oysters, 33; of elephant
tusks, 32; of fish, xvii. *See also*
hunting
overkill hypothesis, 24–25
oysters, eastern, 33

paleontology, 4, 8–9, 13–14
Palila bird, 131, 133
parasitism, 64
Passmore, John, 80
Pechmann, J. H. K., 47
Peirce, Charles Sanders, 83
personal computers, 13
philosophy. *See* environmental ethics

Philosophy and Public Affairs (journal),
78
policymaking: convergence hypothesis
and, 90–94; pressing needs and,
151; process of, 120–24; scientific
evidence and, 150
politics: biodiversity and, 124–25,
140–42; international cooperation
and domestic, 157; lack of universal
valuation and, 160
pollution, 41
population, human, 39, 151
pragmatism, in environmental ethics,
82–84, 91, 92–93
private property rights. *See* property
rights
product information, 71
progress, evolution and, 15–18
property rights, 134–37, 139, 141,
159–60
public goods, 112–13
punctuated equilibrium, 16–17

rain forests. *See* tropical forests
Ramsar Convention (1971), 153
Raup, David, 18–19, 22
Reagan, Ronald, 132
Red List of Threatened Species (IUCN
Red List), 43–45
Redbook (endangered species list), 127
Regan, Tom, 84–85, 87
regulations, 121
research: future of, 49; history of, 31–32
reserves, ecological, 35
Respect for Nature (Taylor), 86
rock record, time determined by, 8–12
Rolston, Holmes, III, 86–87, 88–89
Routley, Richard, 79–81

Sand County Almanac, A (Leopold), 79
Savannah River Ecology Laboratory
(SREL), 48
Sepkoski, John, 13–14

shrimp, harvesting of, xvii
Sierra Club, 131
Silent Spring (Carson), 41
Simberloff, D. S., 22
Singer, Peter, 84–85, 88–89
Smallwood, Jeffrey A., 48
Smith, Adam, 110
Smith, William, 8
snail darter, 130
songbirds, 55–71; background on, 57–58; habitat changes for, 61–67; population monitoring of, 59–60; as research subject, 56
species: classification of, 12–13, 48; evolution of new, 21–22; introduction of, 40, 76–77; inventories of, 46
species evenness, 34
species richness, 34
Sterba, James, 86
Supreme Court, U.S., 130, 131
sustainable development, 158
swans, mute, 75–77, 93–94

taxonomy. *See* classification of organisms
Taylor, Paul, 86
Tellico Dam, 129–31
Tennessee Valley Authority (TVA), 129–30
time: geological, 7–8, *10*; rock record of, 8–12

Toward Unity among Environmentalists (Norton), 90
trade in vulnerable species, 155–57
tropical forests: biodiversity in, 22–23; rate of loss of, 149–50

United States Agency for International Development, 66
unsustainable use of species. *See* overharvesting
utilitarianism, in environmental ethics, 82, 85

valuation: economic, 104–8; ethical, 87–94; lack of universal, politics resulting from, 160
Varner, Gary, 86
Vermont Fish and Wildlife Department, 76–77, 93

Ward, Peter, 21
Westra, Laura, 91–92
wetlands, 153–54
Wilbur, H. M., 47
Wilson, E. O., 22
World Conservation Union, 43–45

Yellowstone National Park, 154

zebra mussels, 40–41
zoocentrism, 84–85